#1 CODE BREAK BOY

Communications Intelligence in the Korean War

John Milmore

ISBN 0-7414-1246-2

Published by:

519 West Lancaster Avenue
Haverford, PA 19041-1413
Info@buybooksontheweb.com
www.buybooksontheweb.com
Toll-free (877) BUY BOOK
Local Phone (610) 520-2500
Fax (610) 519-0261

Printed in the United States of America

Printed on Recycled Paper

Published September, 2002

Table of Contents

Dedication

To the mostly teen-age enlisted men of Army Security Agency who served anonymously during the Korean War this book is dedicated. Firstly, the radio intercept operators who tracked elusive enemy transmissions and copied for hours meaningless morse code numbers and letters - never knowing if it had any value. Secondly, to the Teletype and crypto operators who relayed the intercepts to higher headquarters keeping meticulous attention to detail. Lastly, to all other members of the team; analysts, security guards, cooks, truck drivers, equipment repairmen and other support personnel - their efforts were not in vain. As far as the officers were concerned, aside from almost all translators and a handful of traffic analysts, their performance was terrible.

Preface

This is a story concerning an organization of the United States Army that the government is reluctant to admit ever existed. It was known as the Army Security Agency. Its primary mission was to provide communications intelligence - that is to intercept enemy radio messages and derive as much information as possible by either decoding the material or from the traffics` external characteristics, such as pin-pointing the source of the transmission. The secondary mission was to construct, distribute and maintain secure cryptographic systems to other American military units as well as the Department of State.

Most histories that pertain to "code-breaking" involving the Pearl Harbor Disaster are replete with excuses, denials and conflicting versions. However, after the American entry into World War II, the narratives are heavy with yarns of self-sacrificing heroics, officer idolatry, and statements to the effect that the allies could not have won the big world war without such amazing efforts. Korea was a different story. This is the only true firsthand narrative you will hear. There is an "official" or otherwise constructed legend, developed by "Historians" of The National Security Agency. This chronicle, as seen through the eyes of the principle cryptanalyst involved, depicts the situation prior to the North Korean onslaught and first year of conflict, including the Chinese participation.

Every account of World War II communications intelligence has a spooky title with words such as "ULTRA", "TOP SECRET", "MAGIC", "ENIGMA" and so on. The only synthetic word to fit the Korean War would be "GIZMO", a term of unknown origin that signifies a gadget. On the morning of June 25, 1950, somewhere in Japan, an uncelebrated enlisted man, either a morse radio intercept operator or a traffic analyst, applied "GIZMO" to the torrent of messages that erupted from the North Korean Peoples Army. In order for intercepted messages to fit into the bureaucratic stream it must possess a five-letter, pronounceable code word that identifies the country of origin. North Korean traffic was not targeted for monitoring, so no code word existed. The concocted "GIZMO" was the designation used by the four Army Security Agency radio intercept stations located in Japan - Tokyo, Kyoto, Chitose (Hokkaido) and Futema (Okinawa). The superb U. S. Navy Radiomen of World War II were in dry dock and the infant Air Force Security Service had yet to get off the ground. A few weeks into the "Police Action", to avoid confusion with intercepts from other sources and to confirm official approval an eminently forgettable code word was applied to North Korean communications. Too bad - "GIZMO" was more appropriate to the rag-tag intelligence operation that was underway.

The only substantial reference to code breaking and communications-intelligence relevant to this book is page 179 in "Korea - The Forgotten War" by Clay Blair. The information came to the author of that book "over the transom", so he should not be held accountable for its validity. Other attempts at depicting COMINT rely on selectively released declassified reports that were originally incomplete, self-serving and inaccurate. This includes the feeble attempts by "official historians" of the National Cryptologic Museum. Throughout history there has been a shroud of mystique surrounding code breaking, or more properly cryptanalysis. The obvious reason for this secrecy is to prevent your adversary from becoming aware that you are reading his mail. However, the U. S.

government, as well as the British has raised the mysterious factor to an art form.

In May of 1950 a law was promulgated - "The Communications Intelligence Security Act" (U. S. C., Title 18, Section 798). It was just in time to blot out information on this subject concerning the Korean and "Cold" wars, as well as prevent any inquiry into failures, incompetence, malfeasance in office and dereliction of duty. This statutory answer to a government bureaucrat's dream has never been tested as to its constitutionality, although it flies in the face of the first amendment.

There was a little girl,
Who had a little curl,
Right in the middle of her forehead,
When she was good,
She was very, very good,
But when she was bad she was horrid.

This little limerick more aptly describes communications intelligence, also known as COMINT, cryptanalysis or codebreaking. When it fails it is disastrous. The list of fiascoes is long; "Pearl Harbor", "Tonkin Gulf", The Korean War as described in this account, and lamentably the events of September 11, 2001. In July 1995 there was a attempt to maintain the magical aura of code-breaking intelligence with the joint Central Intelligence Agency-National Security Agency "VENONA" release of translations of decryption's of Soviet messages that purport to "prove" the guilt of the Rosenbergs, Alger Hiss and other assorted malefactors. The only thing that is "proven" is the candidacy for the longest running government boondoggle in the annals of boondogglery - 1943 to 1980.

Since the publication of various "Ultra Secrets" in the 1970's, when it was propounded that the solving of the German "Enigma" encryption machine shortened World War II by six months. Other recent cryptologic books by the chronologists of the late Great Britain now say the war was actually shortened by two and half years. If this trend continues there will be no history of the war, but only the heroic efforts of those at Bletchley Park. In most of these books no mention is ever made concerning the initial cryptanalysis of ENIGMA by the Polish Government.

Cryptanalysis is analogous to solving a crossword puzzle. There is nothing really super-human or occult about it. True, an extensive knowledge of the technology is necessary, but no more than contemporary requirements for adequate computer "literacy". Military code-breaking or puzzle solution is relatively easy when the daily crossword puzzle changes, but the words remain the same.

An important aspect of this narrative is the existence of over two hundred easily decipherable intercepted messages from the North Korean Army that preceded the attack of June 25, 1950. There are two parts to this circumstance, one naturally is why wasn't this done at the time of intercept and appropriate diplomatic or military action taken to prevent the invasion. The second is why weren't these messages translated and forwarded to higher headquarters not too long after they were collected as they still contained very valuable intelligence information.

The first situation can easily be explained away by the limited communications intelligence resources available including lack of Korean translators and the failure to specify North Korea as an intelligence target. Furthermore, the United States military was in a deplorable condition at the time. The one mobile infantry division, the 82nd airborne stationed at Ft. Bragg, North Carolina, took almost three months to prepare and could only muster one regiment when ordered to Korea. Secondly, although the U. S. Air Force had B-29 bombers based in Japan, there were no nuclear weapons on hand, ruling out any posturing with weapons of mass destruction as was done during the Berlin airlift crisis of 1948.

The second instance, the failure to translate and produce the pre-war decrypts was a case of malfeasance in office and dereliction of duty. The civilian team from the Armed Force Security Agency (the predecessor of NSA) as well as responsible Army Security Agency officers colluded in this decision. This was simply done to preclude a "Pearl Harbor" type investigation, either by legislative committees or by the president. It would be very difficult to estimate the amount of American casualties that resulted by this act of deliberate bureaucratic negligence.

Most of the material in this book was previously classified Top Secret. On April 17th, 1995 President William Clinton signed Executive Order #12958 automatically declassifying anything contained in records that are more than 25 years old, whether or not the records have been reviewed. However, governmental agencies were given five years to examine information to determine if there were exceptions to the declassification order. This time was extended for another year and half.

This story covers the period October 1949 thorough October 1951 - the prelude to the Korean War, the first year of fighting up-and-down the peninsula, and the first months of the stalemate. There will be some flashbacks, as well as flash-forwards to subsequent events. Technical digressions, unfortunately, are necessary to authenticate the account. Most arcana will be found in the appendices, as well as documentation of the efforts of the National Security Agency to prevent publication of this book or preclude availability of any supportive information.

John Milmore
Post Office Box 1632, FDR Station
New York, New York 10150

Chapter I

October 1949 through January 1950
-Arrival in Japan
- First Days on the Job
- Russian Codebreaking

-The author, Richard Copeland and Jack LaDove ASA School, Carlisle Barracks, Pennsylvania upon receiving orders to report to Tokyo, Japan August 1949.

On Sunday, October 23rd 1949 the Army Transport Ship General William Frederick Hase docked in Yokohama, Japan, after a leisurely trip across the calm Pacific Ocean from San Francisco. It was loaded with soldiers and military dependents bound for occupation duty in Japan. A small group of 16 soldiers, led by a sergeant, were the first to disembark. Two trucks were waiting on the dock to take them directly to their duties at General MacArthur's Headquarters - Far East Command in Tokyo. They were Army Security Agency (ASA) personnel under the assignment jurisdiction of the Chief of Staff for Intelligence (G-2) of the General Staff of the United States Army. The group included the Sergeant in charge Al Wight who was a Russian language translator just out of the Army Language School at Monterey, California. Within the group were three young cryptanalysis technicians (code breakers) fresh out of the Army Security Agency school at Carlisle Barracks, Pennsylvania Richard Copeland age 19, Jack LaDove a twenty year old, and myself age 18.

The two hour trip was a bit bumpy from Yokohama to the northern part of a still bomb devastated Tokyo to a section called Oji. We arrived at our new home in the early afternoon just in time for lunch - it was a Sunday and roast chicken was on the menu. The mess hall had small four person tables with service provided by young Japanese waitresses who frequently giggled. We ran into two schoolmates from the Crypt-tech class just before ours - Ed Anderson and John LaForge. They told us that we were expected and would be at work within a week. We had arrived at ASAPAC or shorthand for Army Security Agency Pacific.

The American occupied army post was the former First Tokyo Arsenal of the Japanese Imperial Army's Ordnance Corps comprised of many large red brick factory type buildings - some just burnt-out twisted hulks and others completely untouched by the B-29 air raids. The troops were billeted in three apartment like buildings - the ground floors had the orderly room, enlisted mess hall, and supply rooms, dispensary and the officer's mess. The second and third floors had various size squad rooms for from two to eight men, depending on rank. One building was the bachelors officers quarters (BOQ) with triple, double and single occupancy rooms, although the vast majority of officers and sergeants lived with their families at a nearby sprawling military housing area known as "Grant Heights" or at commandeered hotel accommodations.

We were initially assigned to a large room containing about thirty army cots that was affectionately dubbed the "Snake Pit". It was the casual barracks for personnel in transit or awaiting assignment - where the men would return from their first night outings in the local environs that involved consumption of Japanese food, beer, and sake and then they would frequently regurgitate the undigested residue onto the floor.

Highlights from the "Pacific Stars and Stripes" during the month of October 1949, the "hometown" newspaper of the occupation troops in Japan.

- Casey Stengel to stay with the Yanks
- Payment in Yen is now required by all occupation personnel on all trains
- China is lost to communism as the Nationalists abandon Canton.
- The movie of the month "Streets of Laredo" with William Holden.
- Lefty O'Doul and the San Francisco Seals arrive for an exhibition tour against GI and Japanese teams, Gen. MacArthur lunches with the team
- Shirley Temple divorces John Agar
- General Omar Bradley calls Navy Admirals spoiled brats in latest service unification spat
- The Korean Army of 100,000 men is prepared to handle any invasion by the North Koreans, says Brig. Gen. William L. Roberts of the Korean Military Advisory Group (KMAG), the last 500 American Soldiers remaining in Korea.

On October 28th we were assigned to the cryptanalysis section of the Operations Branch, Headquarters Army Security Agency - Pacific. The Chief of ASAPAC was Lieutenant Colonel Morton A. Rubin. The head of the operations branch was Major Clayton S. Swears. Both were experienced intelligence officers.

The cryptanalysis section at the time consisted of two officers Captain Richard Ligon and First Lieutenant Elinora Toft, both former schoolteachers. Four cryptanalytic technicians; PFC Edward Anderson, PFC James Fitzmaurice, PFC Richard Dugan and PFC John LaForge, and clerk-typist PFC Marvin L. Fischer rounded out the section. The four crypt techies were from the class that preceded us at ASA School at Carlisle Barracks, Pa.

The section was in a small room on the second floor of white concrete building. Across the hall was the translation section under Captain Jack "Happy Jack" Apollony. This included newly arrived Russian translator Sgt. Al Wight, and temporarily the above named crypt techs had desk space there.

The three of us were furnished with tiny wooden desks that were designed for average Japanese men and crammed into a small room with the two officers and the clerk-typist.

Capt. Ligon gave us a very brief rundown on their current efforts. "We are reading the traffic of the Ninth and Tenth Russian Air Armies. They use a one-part three-digit code. They re-encipher with additive from a five-hundred group page that they change every month." That was it. Our job responsibility was the ninth Air Army. I was given the traffic for the month of September, Jack got August and Cope received July. We were given one copy of the partially recovered codebook - less than a third of the 300 possible code values. We took turns making our individual copies of the Russian Cyrillic entries - on-the-job education in the Russian language.

We usually worked with the Teletype copies of the intercepted messages. There were three radio intercept stations spread throughout the Japanese islands located in Kyoto, Okinawa, and Chitose (Hokkaido) and also from several mobile locations occasionally dispatched from Tokyo. Intercepted traffic was transmitted to ASAPAC in Tokyo then relayed to Arlington Hall, Virginia - the headquarters of Army Security Agency.

RUAMT-3 was the designation for the cryptosystem the was employed for operations of the 9th Russian Air Army that was Headquartered in Vozdevezhenka, 95 Kilometers north of Vladivostok, in the Soviet Union's Maritime Province. The 9th was the air force complement of the Russian occupation of North Korea above the 38th parallel of latitude. They had bases in Hamhung, Wonsan, Chongjin, Pyongyang, and Sinuiju, as well as the Manchurian locales of Harbin, Mukden (Shenyang), Dairen and the Old Russian naval base at Port Arthur. In their codebooks the Russians used the transliterated Japanese names for the localities, rather than the actual Korean - Keijo for Pyongyang.

The daily traffic usually consisted of the air base duty officer reporting the arrival or departure of aircraft. Our job was to determine the additive, neatly print it out on graph paper, as well as the enciphered text, the plain codebook number and the transcribed Russian lettering. The graph paper was trimmed, stamped TOP SECRET plus a five-letter code word (either "ACORN" or "COPSE" at that time MAGIC and ULTRA had expired) and with the original message, paper-clipped and placed on the Captain's Desk by 4:30 every day. The decryptions were then reviewed and passed across the hall to the translation section, There they were again reviewed, translated and the typed multipart English versions were stamped TOP SECRET - Code Word. One copy was filed with the original message and the graph paper decryption. Other translation copies were forwarded by courier to General MacArthur's Intelligence (G-2) section and to Arlington Hall, Virginia - from there it was then delivered to the Commanding General - Chief of Staff for Intelligence at the Pentagon.

The use of "additive" involves using non-carrying addition. That is, only the single digits are employed with no carry over. The inverse, or decryption, is by subtraction. Somehow, this process became known as GI arithmetic. A typical decoded message would look something like this:

Message __034 945 963 562 500 186 735 467 270 613

Additive__.062 ___ 895 406 462 018 524 246 108 659

PlaCode__.072 ___ 178 166 148 178 211 221 172 064

Russian Cyrillic Characters ______________________>>

The below English equivalent was not included:

Reporting _____ 3 Air- 1 3 Hours 6 Sept. Duty

the Takeoff Craft Officer

The second three-digit group of the message was the key or indicator group. It was supposed to tell where on the additive page that the encryption would begin. We never figured out how it worked. The encipherment of the indicator group usually was an involved process that changed daily, if not hourly. This message specific key is, in theory, the strength of any cryptographic system.

Knowledge of the keying system was unnecessary for several reasons, the main one being that the Soviet officers were neglectful and frequently started enciphering on page 1, line 1, column 1 of the 500 group additive page. The second reason was that messages could be placed "in depth", that is enciphered by the same segment of additive, by observing identical code groups between messages, or "hits", that indicate duplicate code-book values enciphered by the same additive.

[A further explanation of this analytic process and Russian cryptographic systems is found in David Kahn`s "The Codebreakers", page 440, see bibliography.]

We plunged into the code-breaking process with all the enthusiasm of youngsters just out of school, which in realty we were, and were soon turning out decryptions with carefully calligraphed Russian script. Progress was measured slowly as only three or four additive groups were recovered each day using the laborious "trial and error" method. The atmosphere in the small office was comparable to a classroom or library - no conversation. Any collaborative effort or discussion was met with a scornful, glare from Captain Ligon. When he was absent from the room, which was frequent, we were able to compare notes and increase production.

One auspicious day I chanced upon a long message that was an inventory of aircraft at a particular air base. It spelled out, letter-by-letter, the nickname or manufacturer of each model following the identification such as YAK-3 YAKOLEV including "lend-lease" American aircraft that had been delivered to the Soviets during WWII - like the P-47 "Thunderbolt". After the designation P-39 there was a long gap in the message that was the result of unrecovered additive. I immediately assumed it was "Aircobra" the designation given by Bell Aircraft. Almost every boy who grew up during WWII was familiar with the widely distributed illustrations and identification silhouettes of aircraft used by Allies and Axis alike, including decks of special playing cards and cards enclosed in bubble-gum packages.

I plugged in the Russian spelling AEROKOBRA, recovered nine more additive groups and was able to decrypt an additional dozen messages. Captain Ligon was impressed, but could not believe the AEROKOBRA designation. Captain Appolony, in charge of Russian translation confirmed it to the embarrassment of Ligon. It was becoming apparent that Captain Ligon's military knowledge of both Russian and American nomenclature was superficial, as well as his depth in cryptography. That night Jack, Dick and myself celebrated in the enlisted men's club my nineteenth birthday, our accomplishments in our new occupation and the embarrassment of Ligon, who we were rapidly losing respect for.

Further gleanings from the "Pacific Stars and Stripes" for November 1949. - Former Secretary of State Stettinius dies of heart attack

- "Japan to get Peace Treaty in 1950 - MacArthur"
- Herbert H. Leahman beats John Foster Dulles for Senator in New York, the only newsworthy event of the off-year election

Welfare State Democrats versus "against the end of liberty and wasteful government spending" Republicans.

- Britain to recognize Red China
- American consul Ward in Mukden arrested by communists
- Jackie Robinson voted most valuable player in baseball
- Vice President Alben Barkley marries the Veepess
- Chunking Falls - Senator Knowland in Tokyo says that China can be saved
- Thanksgiving weekend football Army 38 Navy 0 - Notre Dame 32 USC 0
- Tokyo Masonic Lodge honors Macarthur aide Colonel Huff and Eighth Army's General Walton Walker
- The movie of the month- "Any Number Can Play" with Clark Gable and Alexis Smith.

Although there was much activity in China our communications intelligence activities were aimed at Soviet Russia. The codebreaking and translation slipped into a daily routine, with Jack and myself taking off three afternoons a week to practice with the post basketball team. We were becoming adjusted to Japan, delving into the Japanese Language when off-duty while engrossed in the Russian Language during working hours.

The Russian translator, Sergeant Al Wight and myself started working on an novel encryption system that we hoped ASA would accept, or alternatively we could market for commercial purposes. We proceeded to spend a lot of time in the endeavor, including Saturdays or Sundays in the office or at Al's home in the military housing facility nearby called "Grant Heights".

On Christmas day members of the cryptanalysis class immediately behind ours arrived in Japan including Reilly, Foley, Wall, Hawkins and Sgt. Schmock. Dick Copeland and myself were on the dock in Yokohama to greet them and escort them to Tokyo in time for a Christmas dinner - complete with entertainment by a Japanese string quartet. The crypt section was now expanded to over a dozen people situated in a much larger accommodation. We now occupied a 20 by 30-foot room, with space for four rows of five desks each. The desks were still tiny. Jack, who was six foot two inches tall, frequently upset his.

The space that we now occupied was vacated by the Traffic Analysis Section, which now possessed the entire upper floor of "B" building. ASA Tokyo was arranged oddly enough like a little Arlington Hall, the location of ASA's headquarters just outside Washington in Virginia. Both posts had a Headquarters building, and two additional work buildings "A" and "B". Barbed wire fences surrounded the “A” and “B” buildings. Entrance was permitted only through a gate manned twenty-four hours by security guards.

Traffic analysis is that branch of signal intelligence analysis, which deals with the study of the external characteristics of signal communications for the purpose of obtaining information concerning the organization and operation of an adversary's communication system. The data is used (1) as a guide to efficient intercept operation, (2) as an aid to cryptanalysis, and (3) as a basis for drawing deductions and inferences of value as intelligence even in the absence of specific knowledge of the contents of the message. This is the textbook definition. In actual practice, when a bureaucracy or "command structure" is established human nature takes over and teamwork fades and trivial competition begins.

Not only were we prohibited from talking to translators, but also there was absolutely no liaison with traffic analysts. We never had any idea of the identity of Russian Air Force call signs, message priorities or radio direction finding "fixes" that would supply information helpful in decoding messages. We worked completely in the dark. This policy of "compartmentalization", either for contrived security reasons or simple empire building, was seriously impacting productivity.

Below is a fragment from a declassified Russian three-digit codebook. The German Army in World War II captured it. This part lists airports at various localities. Code value numbers 287 and 290 are Moscow, 332 Orel and 343 Odessa.

283 ЛОВОЗЕРО
285 ЛИВНЫ
286 ЛИБАВА
287 **МОСКВА** (Центральный аэродром)
290 МОСКВА (ИЗМАЙЛОВО)
291 МЕЛИТОПОЛЬ
293 МАЛАЯ ВИШЕРА
295 МИРГОРОД
327 **ОБОЗЕРСКАЯ**
330 ОКУЛОВКА
332 ОРЕЛ
334 ОСТАШКОВ
337 ОРДЖОНИКИДЗЕ
341 ОПОЧКА
343 ОДЕССА
345 ОРША

Items from December 1949 - "Pacific Stars and Stripes"

- Earthquake jars Tokyo on Christmas day, 8 deaths
- Gen. MacArthur frees 46 Japanese war criminals in a Christmas amnesty
- Rita Hayworth presents Aly Kahn with 5 1/2 pound princess
- India, Canada and Australia follow Britain's recognition of Red China
- Chiang Kai-shek flees to Formosa
- Cleveland Browns beat San Francisco 21-7 for the American Football Conference Championship
- Jerusalem chosen as capital by Israel in defiance of the United Nations
- Alger Hiss on trial for perjury in New York
- 720th Military Police Battalion beats Arsenal (the unofficial name of Army Security Agency Pacific a.k.a. ASAPAC) 37-23 in GHQ League Basketball
- Clark Gable weds Lady Sylvia Ashley, widow of Doug Fairbanks
- Armed Forces to cut 8,000 reserve officers from active duty - Defense Secretary Louis Johnson on Dec. 7th said Pearl Harbor will not happen again.

- ASAPAC beats 441st Counter Intelligence Corps Detachment 34-19 in basketball
- Movie: "Task Force" with Gary Cooper and Jane Wyatt.

Chapter II

January through May 1950
- The use of IBM equipment to break a Russian Code -
  - Temporary assignment to Traffic Analysis Section -
  - Mystery messages from North Korea -
  - Run up to the North Korean Attack –

ASAPAC Headquarters building as it appears today.

The trial-and-error method of attacking Russian coded traffic that we were using is extremely time consuming. The technique is first placing messages "in depth", that is assuming segments are enciphered using the same additive "key", then making a further assumption - a code value, then proving the supposition by getting valid code values in the other in depth message or messages. The rule-of-thumb - at least three valid code entries, "in depth" and in coherent text, must be demonstrated before the additive is deemed recovered.

A more efficient procedure that we were trained in at ASA School is called "differencing". This is based on the fact that the arithmetic "non-carrying" difference between any two plain code groups is the same even when an identical additive encrypts them. Example: the 9th Air Army (RUAMT-3) code value for "duty officer" number 064 is subtracted from the value for "Yakolev-3" number 287 giving a difference of 223. If both code values are encrypted with the additive quantity 222 the results 286 and 409 still have the same difference 223.

Accordingly, I constructed a small "difference table" of the 25 most frequently used recovered code values in the 9th air army's codebook, yielding a table of 300 entries. [formula for the number of entries in a difference table: (N(N-1))/2 or (25 times 24) divided by 2 = 300].

I shared this small difference table with LaDove and Copeland and it resulted in a marked increase in our productivity. Captain Ligon noticed this, was only vaguely familiar with the technique, but asked me to explain it. I pointed out that the process for constructing a difference table is usually done using IBM punched card machines that were available at ASA headquarters back at Arlington Hall and they may have already constructed tables that would be of value to us. I went over the solution procedure and without further discussion he decided to construct a similar table for the Russian 10th air army's codebook.

The 10th was generating much more traffic then the ninth. Its headquarters was in Karborovsk and stretched across the entire Soviet Far East with bases in Magadan, on the island of Sakhalin, the Kamchatka

Peninsula and all the way to Provadenyia - opposite Alaska. They were using a codebook of 1000 entries, with only about half fully recovered.

All 808's (the military occupation specialty { MOS} designation for cryptanalysis technician) except for myself were then employed in constructing this difference table. Captain Ligon systematically parceled out to all batches of 3 by 5 index cards to determine the differences of the 500 recovered code groups. He hadn't realized that this would entail 250,000 cards.

Consequently, all the traffic for the 9th Russian Air Army (RUAMT-3) became my responsibility. This included September 1949 and previous as well as October and November 1949 which had been untouched up till now. It was all unceremoniously dumped on my desk.

There were about 400 messages for the month of October. Rather then wade through all this traffic looking for "hits", then using the differencing technique, I hit upon another method. Since the initial digit of the three-digit codebook was limited to 0-1-2, then as a result of being enciphered with the same digit the result must be similarly limited. Example - if the additive digit was seven, then the enciphered code digit had to be 7, 8 or 9.

I took all the traffic and with a scissors trimmed off all of the excess paper on the top and bottom of the messages. I then sorted all of the traffic on the first digit of the initial group. Then keeping them in sequence I sorted on the first digit of the third group (The second group was the enciphered message indicator or starting point on the additive page). Then I sorted on the initial digits of the fourth group and stopped there.

By now several messages had fully identical groups - "Hits" in cryptanalytic jargon, indicating that the messages were probably enciphered with the same additive key. Using assumptions of the standardized Russian text, the messages were decoded, about twenty additive groups recovered and the codebook value for the Russian language word for the month of October identified.

If an assumed code book value occurs at least three times in coherent text and appears in the codebook in proper alphabetic sequence it is considered recovered. Actually, there is a nebulous value scale from A to D indicating the validity of a recovery. It was never fully rationalized and there was considerable disagreement with Arlington Hall in this matter. Hence, translations would occasionally differ.

The procedure of aligning the messages proved effective, but sorting all these scraps of Teletype paper was unwieldy. If someone opened a window, a breeze would put most on the floor and disrupt the process. It was time to put the machines to work.

Recently, an IBM tabulating unit had arrived from the states. It consisted of two IBM 405 Accounting Machines plus the auxiliary machines sorters, reproducers, collators and several key-punch machines. The men assigned to operate and maintain the equipment arrived several months previous and were performing various temporary jobs.

In theory all sections should have access to this facility, but it became a political football. The Security Section used it for their accounting of Cryptographic Material - a high priority item. Traffic Analysis used it for various applications; Direction Finding (D/F), correlating traffic identification and so on. The Personnel Section got their oar in the water with duty rosters. All the above were simple applications or had pre-wired control panels and procedures sent from Arlington Hall.

The Cryptanalysis Section, which was the original intended user of the IBM unit, became the orphan. No procedures, no control panels (plugboards), no experienced staff, but most importantly no knowledgeable cryptanalytic officers were on hand.

I outlined a procedure based upon what we had been taught in class and approached Ligon. I explained the process, stressing that it would not work for the 10th Air Army because that was a full-blown 1000 group code. He had been impressed with the recoveries and translations for the 9th Air Army October traffic so far. Surprisingly, he said go ahead meanwhile he curtailed the scope of the difference table that he was using everybody else to construct.

It was like pulling teeth trying to get the job done. Although, some of the men in the IBM unit were off-duty drinking buddies the priority given to the project was the lowest. Pfc.'s cannot out pull Captains and Majors, although the primary purpose of the IBM unit was an aid to cryptanalysis. The traffic for October was keypunched and after a week I received a bulky IBM printout on four-part paper with interleaved carbons. That was all they had in stock. After decollating the paper I was able to roll-up the full 500 group additive page and be in a position to decode the entire month's traffic.

Ligon took Dick Copeland and Jim Fitzmaurice from the difference table project to expedite the decoding. In the process, "Fitz" caught on to something. He noticed that some of the additive groups had also appeared in the page for another month's traffic. Sure enough, a line of additive appeared down a column on alternating lines from a month he previously worked on. This indicated that the Soviets were using some form of transposition technique to generate their additive pages from month to month.

At this time we received a well-written memorandum from Arlington Hall describing the Soviet Russian Air Force and its activities, equipment and capabilities. This was the first official information on what our principal intelligence target was. We were tasked with being especially alert for the word "turbina", Russian for jet engine, as well as any long-range bomber activity. The jet fighters MIG-13 and MIG-15 had recently made their appearance in Europe, but had not been identified as being in the Soviet Far East as yet. The same for the TU-4 (Tupolev), a four engined long range bomber. It seems that during World War II three B-29's flying out of China made emergency landings in the Russian maritime province, near Khaborovsk or Vladivostok. The Russians interned the aircrews, as there was no war between Japan and the U. S. S. R. at the time. They kept the three B-29's, used one for reference, another for training pilots and dissected the third to make a rivet-for-rivet copy. How many they now had flying or in production were a big unknown. Also, how the high-performance jet fighters such as the MIG-15 and American F-86 would do against the B-29 and its look-alike was also a big question. We would find out before the year was out.

In April of 1950 I was detailed to the Traffic Analysis Section for several weeks. A two months backlog of unidentified intercepted messages had accumulated. It was a mixture of original intercept multicolored carbon copies and canary yellow Teletype messages that had been relayed from any of our three intercept stations. It had to be sorted and classified

I was given a desk on the second floor of "B" building an old rickety wooden gloomy two- story Japanese structure. The first floor housed the IBM section and the non-morse intercept operators, that is voice or Teletype interception.

The officer in charge of handling unidentified messages, Lt. Berglund, was a career alcoholic who had trouble focusing his eyes after a three martini lunch at the officer's mess, let alone being able to differentiate between Chinese communist and Soviet traffic. The preponderance of the material was Soviet Russian, readily identified by its characteristic three digit groups for Air Force or five digit groups for Army units. Chinese on the other hand was usually four- digit, reflecting the venerable Chinese Telegraphic Code (CTC). Additionally, Chinese signal procedure differed markedly from the Soviet. Radio direction finding (D/F), although rudimentary and uncoordinated at this time, was also helpful in classification of the unidentified traffic.

After a week or two the backlog was eliminated, except for a batch of four-digit traffic, having Soviet signal procedures and gibberish for apparent plain-text chatter between radio operators. More striking to me as a cryptanalyst was the repetition of the same code groups within a message and among many messages. This would indicate that the cryptosystem was not re-enciphered using the numeric additive methodology - hence easily exploitable. A check of the Chinese Telegraphic Code, and variations, yielded nothing. One D/F technician suggested the traffic emanated from North Korea. Further traffic analysis classified the messages into four distinct networks, called FE001, FE002, FE003 and FE004. This facilitated future identification, the FE standing for Far East- Unknown. No assigned intercept schedule was put into effect for these networks and only random searching of the radio spectrum would pick up any transmissions. These were duly identified, neatly filed and a copy transmitted to Washington at Headquarters, Army Security Agency Arlington Hall Virginia.

My tour of duty in the Traffic Analysis Section was apparently over as I was told to return to the Cryptanalysis Section during the second week in May. Upon returning, the mysterious four-digit traffic designated FE001, 2, 3 and 4 was brought to the attention of Captain Ligon. I told him that there were four distinct networks, using Russian procedure and messages had been intercepted sporadically since November, It was not Chinese Telegraphic Code, direction finding indicated North Korea as its locale, and it looked breakable with many four digit groups repeated within and between messages. A young Lieutenant in the Traffic Analysis section had been looking at the messages from the cryptanalytic viewpoint. The last item caught Ligon's interest, as it was an encroachment on his bureaucratic territory, so he immediately sent for all the traffic to date.

I resumed working on the Russian 9th Air Army's traffic that was now unbreakable since December 1st 1949, after switching to five- digit groups. The volume had dropped considerably as the Russian forces were supposed to have left North Korea. The initial assumption was that it was truly unbreakable - that is "One Time Pad" encryption.

This was our first Spring in Japan and the weather was great. We were given Wednesday afternoons off for physical exercise and recreation. Most guys opted for softball, baseball, basketball or football. It was still a "jock-strap" army. Copeland and myself bought bicycles and would cycle out of Tokyo into the surrounding rice-paddies. Jack signed-up for track and was running on the GHQ track team. He got every afternoon off to practice running the 400-meter sprint.

Dick Copeland, who had a strong sentiment to make the military a career, suggested we enroll in a correspondence course at the Army Security Agency's School. We drafted and submitted letters of application for the next step in our technical training - "Military Cryptanalysis - Part III - Aperiodic Polyalphabetic Substitution". That was cryptographic talk for attacking machine methods of encipherment. It was also the first step in acquiring credit towards a reserve officer's commission.

It was an easygoing life in the occupation of Japan. Best of all were weekends, if there were no formations, parades, inspections, drills or other "Mickey-Mouse" on Saturday mornings, Friday nights we jumped on a train and headed northwest into the Japanese Mountains. We picked the town of Takasaki, a railroad junction about a hundred miles from Tokyo. It was situated in a valley between two dormant volcanoes, with an active one, Mt. Asama, visible in the distance. It was superb hiking country, with many inexpensive Japanese inns available. It was hedonistic to get away from the Army and the Crypt section for a while.

What was more interesting, the local people had rarely if ever seen an occupation soldier and were either terrorized by us or overly friendly. The area had been bombed only once, in August 1945 with minimal casualties, so there was little animosity towards Americans.

On our weekend trips into the interior of Japan we would also occasionally bump into other soldiers - mainly troopers from the first cavalry division who were stationed north of Tokyo. As typical Americans, or soldiers anywhere, we would compare notes as to our assignments and our feelings toward Japan and the Japanese. They envied us from GHQ in Tokyo as not having to go into the "field" on training maneuvers. We passed ourselves off as translators as our command of Japanese, including rudimentary written, impressed them. We would give them various arcane terms for words or phrases that their girlfriends refused to reveal to them. The troopers appreciated this as their vocabulary usually consisted of about ten Japanese words strung together in a "pidgin" vernacular that they and the Japanese they were in contact with both understood. Many GI's pick up this jargon and used it mockingly with each other. It became habit forming.

One afternoon, Major Swears and two Air Force officers walked into the Crypt section and came directly to my desk. Without even a nod to Captain Ligon, he asked me to verify the validity of a decryption of a Russian 10th Air Army message. The communication was over six months old. I asked, "What was the problem?" Swears said the message has a Soviet aircraft with mechanical difficulties landing somewhere on the Japanese Island of Hokkaido. "I see" I replied and pulled out a notebook that contained the Russian coordinate and independent encryption system that they embedded in their messages to indicate an unnamed locality. I rechecked the additive and said "The coordinates were indeed wrong, about 100 miles off, the actual location is in the southern part of Sakhalin, the former Japanese possession of Karafuto". The two Air Force officers grinned Major Swears laughed and they both thanked me and left with the corrected message. The U. S. Air Force record of protecting the Japanese islands from intruders remained intact.

A few minutes later, an agitated Capt. Ligon came over to me and asked who had made the original decryption. I told him I hadn't noticed. Later that night I told John LaForge it was his boo-boo. He thanked me for covering and said "Ligon double checks everything we do, right?" We both laughed.

The U. S. Air Force equivalent of ASA was the Air Force Security Service or AFSS. Their unit in Japan was the First Radio Squadron Mobile based at Johnson Air Force Base, Irumigawa, Japan - not far from us. Over two dozen new ASA radio intercept operators were temporarily assigned there. Additionally, Air Force enlisted cryptanalysts were delegated to ASAPAC to learn Russian codebreaking techniques. Captain Ligon gave them over to Copeland, LaDove and myself for indoctrination. They had already been promoted to sergeant, while we were still Privates, first class.

After three weeks, Captain Ligon threw up his hands and placed the unidentified "North Korean" traffic on my desk saying "I can't make head or tail out of it, see what you can do with it". This was a significant concession considering the snubbing that Major Swears had just given him. I spent a week studying the messages by taking a statistical analysis of the four digit groups, made some notes and stored the traffic away in my file cabinet.

Chapter III

June and July 1950

- The Korean War - Opening Day -
- Secret Intercept Operation "GIZMO"
- Translation Problems
- Breaking the Codes

Plain text letter:

ㄱ ㄴ ㄷ ㄹ ㅁ ㅂ ㅅ ㅇ ㅈ ㅊ ㅋ ㅌ ㅍ ㅎ ㅏ ㅑ ㅓ ㅕ ㅗ ㅛ ㅜ ㅠ ㅡ ㅣ

01 02 03 04 05 06 07 08 09 10 11 12 13 14 15 16 17 18 19 20 21 22 23 24

Cipher Equivalent:

___North Korean Air Force Encryption System (June 1950)______

This simple enciphering system was the first cryptanalysis of many during during the Korean War. The North Korean Air Force used it for over a year.

On Sunday evening, June 25th, Cope and I returned from Takasaki in the Mountains of Japan. When we approached the company orderly room to sign in we noticed a special edition of "Stars and Stripes" pasted on the open door. A large headline blared "Korea at War".

Reporting to the office Monday morning there was much traffic, apparently plain text, that our intercept operators had pulled in over the weekend. In addition there was some four-digit messages that increased in volume as the week progressed. Since there was no official Secret five-letter code word to identify it as North Korean - somebody, bless his heart, came up with GIZMO. A gizmo is a slang word for a gadget or device and its origin is unknown. Code word operation GIZMO was applied to the traffic coming in from our three intercept stations in Hokkaido, Kyoto and Okinawa.

GIZMO didn't last long as Arlington Hall came up with something more readily forgettable.

Arlington Hall also came through with a summation of some of the plain text messages. North Korean Army Headquarters - designated "Tae Dong Gang" (The river flowing through PyongYang) was directing the advanced headquarters "Han Gang" (the river south of Seoul). No mention was made of the four-digit encrypted messages. "The Hall" also sent a chart of the 24 approximate phonetic Korean equivalents of the Morse code letters that the North Koreans were using. There was no way to transmit the Korean symbols.

During the first week I split the encoded traffic into four groups. The first was a simple two-digit "monoalphabetic" cipher used by the North Korean Air Force. The second was what appeared to be a three digit codebook of a thousand entries (the fourth digit was some type of sum-check). Thirdly there was a short 20 group additive strip that was used to repetitively further encipher some of the code-book messages. The remainder which were lower echelon simple code charts of three or four-digit unit of encipherment, sometimes re-enciphered with the above additive.

The North Korean Air Force consisted of over 60 Ilyushin-10's, many more Yakolevs (Yaks) and other fighters, 72 YAK-18 transports and a handful of Polikarpov PO-2 biplane trainers, later to become know as "bed check Charlie's". In the first few days there was much air activity over Seoul and on June 27th there was a North Korean attack on a Danish ship leaving Inchon harbor with evacuees - three Yak's were shot down by the Americans.

Most of this activity was reported in messages to Pyongyang that we were lucky enough to intercept that were encoded in the simplest of cryptographic systems. Two Russian advisers were mentioned - the first named

"Matveev", the second had a Slavic name mangled beyond recognition in the Korean script.

Other dogfights included 5 yaks attacked by F-82's, 3 shot down; and 8 IL-10's versus 4 "Shooting Star" F-80's, 4 shot down.

Bombing of airfields included a strike on the 28th by 12 B-26's from Ashiya (J-1) on Munsan in North Korea, as well as an attack by Yak-9's on the Suwon strip just used by General MacArthur on his inspection trip. One C-54 transport was destroyed.

After the 30th of June when 18 B-26's hit Pyongyang, claiming damage to 25 NKPA aircraft on the ground the volume of Air Force messages dropped considerably. However, they continued to use the simple encryption system for the first year of the war, with periodic minor changes to the key. It would take less than thirty minutes to break into it.

The 135,000 man North Korean Army attacked with ten divisions split into four spearheads. In the Far West the 6th division was driving down the Ongjin peninsula. The 1st division quickly took Kaesong, in the Ouijongbu corridor the 3rd and 4th divisions, led by a brigade of T-34 tanks were driving towards Seoul. On the East Coast the 5th division hopped-scotched south using amphibious landings to bypass the South Korean units opposing them.

The biggest communications intelligence problem was lack of translators and modern, technical dictionaries. Captain Appolony somehow obtained a copy of "A Korean-English Dictionary" by James Gale, a missionary, published in Yokohama in 1897. It had been derived from a book printed in 1880 by French Jesuit missionary priests "Dictionaire Coreene-Francais". The preface of the English-Korean version stated that it contained "ecclesiastical and canonical" terms, but the word for cannon was the one I was looking for. There were equivalents for minister's vestments - alb, surplice and so forth as well as "old yellow striped tiger" and "young yellow striped tiger", but no entries for airplane, tank or regiment. It was virtually worthless.

Far more valuable was a small pocket size "Korean Phrase Book" published by the War Department in March 27, 1944. It was a technical manual (TM 30-642) of 128 pages classified RESTRICTED. It contained emergency expressions with the approximate pronunciation as well as the Korean script, such as "Throw down your arms! - MOOG-ee-roo! PUHR-yuh" and "Obey or I'll fire! - MAHL AHN TOO-room-yen SAWLT-hay-yah". There was a depiction of the Korean "alphabet" and an insight as to how Korean syllables are formed. A priceless description of both the Chinese and native numbering systems was included, as well as a small English-Korean dictionary of military terms. The first Korean term I extracted from the simple monoalphabetic system used by the North Korean Air Force was "Airplane = Pee-hang-gee". The plain text army messages contained many identifiable military unit designations and titles of officers in command - such as "Senior Colonel Li Hak Ku second corps operations officer".

----- A page from the Phrase Book. -----

English	Pronunciation	Korean Spelling
Cartridge	TAHN-yahk TAWNG	탄약통
Firearm	CHAWNG PAW	총포
Grenade	SOOCH-uk TAHN	수척탄
Gun	CHAWNG	총
Howitzer	YOOT-hahn PAW	유탄포
Mine *(land)*	CHEER-ee	지뢰
Mine *(sea)*	SOOR-ee	수뢰
Mortar	KOOP-haw	구포
Pistol	YOOK-h'yul PAW	육혈포
Rifle	SOO CHAWNG	수총
Shell	PAWT-hahn	포탄
Submachine gun	K'YUNG KEE-gwahn CHAWNG	경기관총

CARS, TANKS, PLANES, SHIPS

English	Pronunciation	Korean Spelling
Accelerator	KAH-sawk-gee	가속기
Aircraft carrier	HAHNG-gawng MAW-hahm	항공모함
Airplane	PEE-hang-gee	비행기
Armor	MOO-jahng	무장
Auto	CHAH-dawng CHAH	자동차
Armored car	CHAHNG-gahp-CHAH-dawng CHAH	장갑자동차
Battery	CHUN-un-jee	전지
Battleship	CHUN-too-hahm	전투함
Biplane	PAWG-yup PEE-hang-gee	복엽비행기
Bomber	PAWK-g'yuk-gee	폭격기
Carburetor	tahn-SAW-hwahg-ee	탄소화기
Cargo ship	HWAH-mool SUN	화물선
Clutch	CHUP-dahn-gee	절단기
Controls	CHAW-jawng-gee	조종기
Cruiser	SOON-yahng HAHM	순양함
Deck	KAHP-hahn	갑판
Destroyer	KOOCH-hook HAHM	구축함

The first week in July, when the American infantry met the North Korean Peoples Army (NKPA) for the first time, we started to receive a copy of GHQ's G-3 operations report stamped SECRET. Captain Ligon gathered everyone in the office to sit around his desk, just like a little schoolroom and proceeded to read us the G-3 report. "On July 7th, a defensive line was established south of Pyongtaek by elements of the 34th RCT" he stopped, then said, "I don't know what RCT means." and looked around. Nobody said anything so I piped up "Regimental Combat Team". Surprisingly he didn't redden and glare at me, but nodded and said "Yes" and continued to read on. Before us was a Captain in army intelligence who was ignorant of the fundamental organization of the U. S. military. No wonder we were getting our tails kicked in Korea.

That was the first and only schoolmaster session. After that a "buck-slip" was attached to the report and it was passed around by rank and pecking order. The entertaining thing about the report was the night-and-day difference between actual operations and what the public relations officers and "combat" journalists related. One "Stars and Stripes" headline shrieked "Artillery Duel Rages All Night", while the operations report stated "three rounds of counter-battery fire were exchanged with a North Korean unit".

We were now receiving intercept material from many sources other than ASA Signal Service companies. In a show of inter service cooperation the U. S. Navy from their unit on an island in Tokyo bay forwarded very neatly copied North Korean messages on blue paper. The nearby AFSS First Radio Squadron Mobile just north of Tokyo at Johnson Air Force Base delivered their contribution. Even the Japanese version of the American Federal Communications Commission sent to ASAPAC hand written copy with very good D/F bearings.

In Early July a two-man civilian team from AFSA (Armed Forces Security Agency) arrived by air from Arlington Hall. They were dispatched in response to a request from General MacArthur. The leader was cryptanalyst Henry "Hank" Herczog, accompanied by Madison Mitchell - traffic analyst. The two hung around for a few weeks to see if they could be of any help. They had brought along a modified typewriter that would accept a normal morse-code keyboard letter and type the equivalent Korean letter/symbol font. This would automate the conversion of plain text intercepts to Korean script. Good idea, but Korean syllables are constructed in a combination of vertical and horizontal "letters". Any typewriter's text is linear and made it difficult for the translators to handle. After a few weeks the machine was placed on an unused desk in a corner and gathered dust the rest of the war. Most of the cryptanalytic enlisted crew who studied Japanese on their own developed the skill to produce the Korean syllables from the morse equivalents as well as from decoded messages, due to the similarity of the two languages. Additionally, we started to receive by daily air-courier messages collected by South Korean intercept operators, who heard the plain language morse code and directly wrote out the Korean script.

The first translator to show up was 1st Lt. Richard Chun, flown in from the 5th Regiment based in Hawaii. He was amiable and sat down by my desk as I showed him some of the decrypted text. He confessed that he was unfamiliar with the whole communications intelligence/crypto/black-chamber specialty. I told him that it is typically Army, nothing to it, with the Generals waiting for a PFC and a First Louie to come up with something. I went over the decoded North Korean Air Force traffic with him. He summarized one short message as "there is a battleship coming across the field. The enemy is advancing."

"Hank" Herczog stopped by to inquire how we were doing. Dick Chun related the text and said that without dictionaries it would require much more work. Hank laughed and Jack, sitting nearby, chimed in with the old army joke about the soldier on guard duty who was asked to recite his general orders by the Captain of the guard. After a perfect rendition, the surprised Captain asked, "What would you do if you observed a battleship coming towards you?" The soldier replied "I would torpedo it, Sir." The Captain said "But where would you get the torpedo?" "The same place you got the battleship, Sir" was the retort. We all guffawed. It sort of set the tone for a more relaxed atmosphere in the office.

Another translator, Captain Youn P. Kim, arrived from his teaching post at the Army Language School in Monterey California. Unfortunately, his Top Secret/cryptologic clearance did not arrive with him. He was temporarily denied access to the enclosed security areas, and a slightly ridiculous expedient was worked out. Pfc. Dugan would strap on his U. S. Army issue 45 caliber pistol and carry plain text messages in a briefcase across the areaway to the headquarters building where Captain Kim had a temporary office. The material would be translated while Dugan waited on guard. He would return, deliver the translations to be typed and pick up a new batch of messages and repeat the cycle. Strange way to run a war. Both Kim and Chun went on to perform laborious translation work and were recipients of the army's Legion of Merit medals.

The North Koreans realizing that the United States military was now opposing them tightened up their communications. Fewer plain text messages were coming in, replaced by encrypted traffic. We had worked twenty-two straight days without a break since the war started. Frequently, we put in twelve-hour shifts, sleeping on cots or on desks at night. New staff was arriving daily.

Those of us familiar with the Japanese "kata-Kana" script quickly picked-up the Korean "Hangul" - three symbols were identical in both languages. We briefed the other cryptanalysis technicians in the technique of the proper order of constructing the "strokes" of Korean syllables - work downward from the upper left hand corner - horizontal strokes first then vertical. This procedure was the same for the Chinese/Japanese ideographs. Most of the men mastered the drill, which made it less complicated for the translators to understand the decrypted messages. Those that didn't fell by the wayside and made coffee became clerks, typists, and messengers or transferred out of the section. The officers, whose sole contact with Japanese culture was limited to a lecture in flower arranging or the frustrating experience of trying to get their young Japanese servant girls to understand how to do things the American way, were unable to grasp the subtleties of Korean. They gradually faded from the picture as the enlisted men ran the decryption section. We bypassed the traffic analysis section and received the intercepts directly from our radio operators, the communications center or the couriers. The traffic was split into plain text or identified known ciphers, distributed equitably and rapidly processed and given to the translators. Unbreakable messages were placed on my desk.

One morning there was a small batch of canary yellow undecipherable messages neatly stacked on my desk as I arrived at eight o'clock for work. The visiting AFSA civilian "Hank" Herczog pulled up a chair and sat down next to me and said, "let's both take a crack at it". The traffic consisted of groups of four numeric digits, with some repeated sequences at both the beginnings and endings of several messages. He said, "it looks like it might be another four digit code". I replied, "The NKPA always transmits their coded messages in four digit groups, but it could be a system using two, three or even variable length units of encryption." Furthermore, I pointed out a pattern of three digit repetitions at the beginnings of several messages. He said, "OK lets do it your way" as we then jointly tabulated the frequency of the three digit groups. I felt like a minor league baseball player undergoing a tryout when the manager says' "OK kid let's see your stuff".

It readily became apparent that it was indeed a three-digit unit of encipherment as there was a marked limitation on the frequencies of the first two digits. I said, "It is probably a simple thirty by ten code chart." I then went over the stereotyped nature of message beginnings with the usual phrase "to comrade the commander of such-and-such unit" as well as the standard date, time and the rank and name of the sender. It was a code chart with two digit entries running down the left side, single digits across the top and about three hundred entries within the chart. The entries in alphabetic sequence include frequently used terms such as regiment, battalion, and all the numerals and letters of the Korean alphabet. Similar in construction to the America's standard "highway patrol" code chart with the frequent transmission ending "10 – 4 (old buddy)."

The solution came rapidly as Herczog looked on in open-mouthed wonder. He then composed a cable to be sent to Arlington Hall describing the code breaking effort at ASAPAC in Tokyo. He further stated that the caliber of the MOS 808 enlisted specialists was very high. There was no comment about the officers.

Not surprisingly his compatriot Madison Mitchell who was an intercept specialist came to the same conclusion about the enlisted traffic analysts and intercept operators.

This AFSA team in conjunction with Arlington Hall reallocated intercept assignments between the services to avoid duplication, as the structure of the North Korean communications network became apparent. The material from the Navy and the Air Force soon dried up at ASAPAC as the services went their separate ways. ASA and the AFSS squabbled over who should monitor the Soviet Air Force for two more years. Army intelligence justifiably had no confidence in the half-grown Air Force COMINT entity.

The two-dozen radio intercept operators that were on loan to the Air Force returned to Tokyo to staff an improvised intercept facility. They included Ed Hall and Al Gregor. Al went on to become trick chief – that is shift supervisor. [Ed later became editor of ASAPAC's reunion group newsletter "The Honeybucket Bulletin".]

When visiting VIP's appeared in the cryptanalysis room under the guidance of Hank Herczog he usually brought them and their assistants to my desk for a briefing on the North Korean cryptographic situation. I developed a well-honed five-minute presentation that wouldn't much change for the next year. Some of the luminaries cleared for Top Secret code-word included General Gavin of WW II 82nd Airborne fame and Navy Commander Jacobi the renowned bridge player. The cryptographic situation at the time never involved technical problems; the major uncertainty of concern was shortage of translators and dictionaries.

I had exhausted the small phrase book as a source of Korean words and was running into a brick wall for further recoveries in the NKPA three-digit codebook. We had many up-to-date Japanese-English and English-Japanese dictionaries at our disposal, so I set out to see if there were any Korean-Japanese dictionaries to be had.

Not having the time luxury to scour the used bookstalls in Tokyo's Kanda district another ploy was tried. I had become acquainted with a former Japanese Army Captain who ran a small bar in the Asukayama neighborhood just outside our post. He was on the "purge list", not being eligible to take part in the post-war Japanese democratic government, but seemed to have some influence in the local community, which had a considerable Korean population. He had never fought against American troops during the recent war - serving in China and Korea. The Soviets captured him and he wasn't repatriated until 1947. If anyone knew about a "Chosen-go-Nihon-go Jibiki" he would.

I stopped by his little bar and ordered a bottle of Asahi beer. We often chatted about military matters, we swapped English and Japanese terms and I often dropped off a copy of the English language "Japan Times" so he could practice his English. He was very proud of his career in the Imperial Army and could not fathom why his forces had been defeated by the teen-age American army that he saw every day. I had to take some mild chiding about how the North Koreans were kicking us all over the place. I told him that a shoeshine man on the post (also a former Imperial Japanese soldier) had said to me "Give us two divisions and we'll be on the Tibet border in a month". He laughed and said "Maybe, two months".

I told him that Korea may be in my future and that I would like to study the language, but there were no modern English-Korean dictionaries. Was there a modern Japanese-Korean "Jibiki" that I could buy. He didn't bat an eye and said "Wakarimashita (understood), Stop by tomorrow".

The next night he had a small inch-thick book, which he handed to me. He smiled as I stumbled through the vocalization of the Korean words on the cover - "Cho Sun U - Il Bon U, Il Bon U - Cho Sun U (Korean-Japanese, Japanese-Korean)". I looked up and read off a few terms in Korean - battalion, division, airplane, steam engine and department. He corrected my pronunciation, as the terms were all of Japanese derivation.

The book was just what was needed. One section was in "HanGul (Korean)" sequence, with a pronunciation in the International Phonetic Alphabet, the part of speech, and the Japanese equivalent, both in kata kana and Kanji (Chinese characters), with many synonyms. The second section was in Japanese Hira Gana sequence, with international pronunciation, part of speech and the Korean script meaning. It was compiled sometime in the forties. "How much?" I asked. He replied in Pidgin English "Presento (no charge)" and pushed it towards me. He said "Consider it the Imperial Japanese Army's contribution to the United Nations campaign against aggression". I thanked him profusely. I had the feeling that he knew exactly what purpose the dictionary would serve.

The local people had an inkling of what ASAPAC was all about as the intercept operators would get drunk and talk to each other in Morse code dits and dahs. Those of us that were familiar with Russian would babble and sing Russian Army marching songs and later some of us would chat away in Korean. Additionally, many of us were fluent in Japanese, and some delved into the written mysteries. Unlike the average GI who absorbed the language from his live-in Japanese girl friend (which had a distinctive feminine grammatical cast), we would expound elegant phrases, as well as the most crude and arcane expressions that only could have come from endless hours perusing large lexicons.

The newly found dictionary proved invaluable, in picking up modern technical terminology. Since it was not of Government Issue and not classified-to-be-locked-in-a-safe, I left it in on my desk when not there. Later, when we were fully staffed with translators, they made frequent trips from their office across the hall to access it. Finally, since I had only an occasional need for it, it was turned over to the translation section, with the proviso that it is returned to me. It eventually disappeared, probably with a translator who was compiling his own dictionary for later private publication.

On July 17th the Chief of ASAPAC Colonel Morton A. Rubin transferred to General Willoghby's intelligence section in the Dai Ichi building (GHQ) in downtown Tokyo. His new duties included a daily briefing of General MacArthur on communications intelligence (COMINT). The new Chief, Army Security Agency Pacific was Colonel Edwin C. Greiner, branch of service Armor, formerly cavalry. He was a West Pointer, carried a riding-crop, wore jodhpurs, and had no intelligence experience whatsoever. He was a "passed-over-full-bird" who would never be promoted to general. Probably because his wife had a "drinking problem" and he was not the sharpest knife in the drawer.

On July 21st, four weeks into the Korean War - having gained a deep insight into the language and cryptographic workings of the North Korean Peoples Army, I recalled the unidentified messages. That night I drew the assignment to do nothing but sit in the

Operations Office on the first floor of "A" building and answer the telephone or call the duty-officer if something of importance occurred.

I dug out the pre-war traffic and carried it downstairs to the office and started to analyze it. It turned out to be a simple substitution system - unique to the syllabic nature of the Korean Language. I decoded a few of the messages, typed a description of the system for transmittal to Washington, and left the remaining sixty messages to be decoded and translated by the staff next day.

At about 11 PM, that night's duty officer Major Swears came by accompanied by the two Department of the Army civilians recently arrived from Washington, Mr. Herczog and Mr. Mitchell. The Major, who was the Chief of the Operations Branch, Intelligence Division, asked if anything was up. I said just routine, but added that I had broken that pre-war "FE" traffic and that it was North Korean. He said good work, lock everything up and that I should take tomorrow off.

Herczog was very interested in the traffic. I asked him why it had not been identified and processed in Washington. He replied everything at Arlington Hall was either Russian "RU" or all others "ALLO". So this "FE" traffic (North Korean) must have fallen between the cracks. He added it also was probably very low on the priority list and that Traffic Analysis in Tokyo was much closer to the problem. He made a note of the transmission dates of the messages - November 1949 through May 1950.

When I returned a day later I inquired if Washington had responded to the solution, as was the usual procedure with a thank you and further comments. Capt. Ligon informed me that the solution was not transmitted and the traffic although completely decoded would not be translated as it is only training messages. I pointed out that it contained base locations, weapons, tactics, personnel, potential air and sea targets, and other valuable information. He stated the matter would not be discussed again and I was further directly ordered never to bring the subject up.

It was obvious that for purely petty bureaucratic reasons a vast collection of valuable intelligence about the North Korean army was to be withheld from the proper commanders. This would have begged the question "Why wasn't this material available six-months ago - or two months ago?" and probably resulted in another "Pearl Harbor" investigation.

This could not have happened if Lt. Colonel Rubin was still in command. I considered "going-over-heads" and bringing this material to his attention at MacArthur's headquarters, thus ending my military career as an underpaid cryptanalyst - Private, First Class. Instead I took the untranslated traffic and stashed it deep in my locked file cabinet. The present war was more important. It was getting personal and close to home as the casualty reports now listed men that I had taken basic training with or had attended the Signal School with us back at Fort Monmouth, NJ.

I could not understand the attitude of the ASA officers or the AFSA civilians, but found the answer later that evening while reading the army newspaper "Stars and Stripes". The lead article was about General Dean, Commander of the 24th Infantry Division, who was reported missing after leading a bazooka squad against T-34 tanks in Taejon. Buried deep in the paper was a tiny article quoting General Dean saying, "My men won't fight, because my officers are no good".

Chapter IV

August and September 1950
- The Pusan Perimeter -
- "001" The North Korean People's Army Codebook -
- The Inchon Landing -
- The Retreat of the North Korean Army --

Sporadically at first, but increasingly so as the front stabilized around the Pusan perimeter the major NKPA command network used a three digit one-part code. The fighting of the I or II Corps was directed by headquarters, either in Pyongyang "Tae Dong Gang" or principally by an advanced "front-line Headquarters" - previously designated in plain text as "Han Gang". Now their transmissions had three-character radio Morse code call signs that were changed periodically - such as CX4, 1B7, 4TG. The "Front Line HQ" was a command echelon in Seoul, but split in August with an advanced HQ displaced to Kumchon.

The division to regiment or battalion networks continued to use either plain text or simple cipher systems. The messages were translated and flashed to General Walker's Eight Army headquarters as soon as possible, enabling him to issue orders for even squads to adjust their positions to counter North Korean movements.

The three-digit code, later found to be designated by the NKPA as "001", was a thousand group "dictionary" code that was in Korean "onmun" (alphabetic) sequence. It had mostly military terminology, as well as the numerals zero through nine, the single letters of the Korean Script and frequently used syllables and place names. It was used throughout the first year of the war as the basis for subsequent additive encryption and derived two-part codes. A two part code is one in which the numeric equivalents are not in the same sequence as the alphabetic "dictionary", rendering it more tedious to use, but much more difficult to successfully cryptanalyze.

The Corps to HQ link used an "additive" key to further encrypt their messages. At first it was just a sequence of 20 groups that repetitively re-encoded the three-digit text. This required little effort to determine and strip off. Later they used a full-blown additive page of 500 groups. In theory a message can use additive starting anywhere on the page, but in bad security practice many messages began using the first group on the page.

Norman Wild, the renowned East-Asian language scholar, arrived to augment the translation process. He was dispatched from AFSA at Arlington Hall and lent a more professional and academic approach to translating that complemented the military specialists. He was fluent in Japanese and Korean, among other languages, as well as Brooklynese - therefore we could communicate easily as we were from the same section of Brooklyn, having attended adjacent High Schools - Midwood and Madison. Other newly arrived translators were Major Linn and a civilian Mr. Erskine St. Clair. We still were lacking in functional dictionaries.

In Early August, as the front stabilized along the Naktong River, which became "The Pusan Perimeter" the North Korean Peoples Army organized into two distinct Corps that reported to advanced headquarters located in Seoul or Kumchon. The Corps commanders in their reports used very long messages that described the locations of all subordinate units as well as the opposing forces. Often these messages would exceed 500 groups, so they would "double back" and use the same additive groups again. This permitted the recovery of the additive by purely mechanical methods - "differences" between frequently used code groups or by assuming stereotypic message endings or beginnings.

The lower echelons without the re-encipherment used the same code. This permitted the recovery of codebook groups that further aided in the reduction of the additive pad. Many of the standardized messages could be completely decoded and translated, but others would be incomplete, with doubtful code book values as complete recovery of the codebook was a tedious translation process, not unlike the solution to a very large crossword puzzle or composing a dictionary.

Kim Il Sung himself came to our rescue with an extremely lengthy, loquacious, message announcing a special meal for August 15th to celebrate the liberation of the Korean homeland from the Japanese. The menu for the commemoration included an item called "Muk Pi" or "Moog Bee", which didn't sound too appetizing to the American taste, but sure helped in the cryptographic war. Since the communication came from the supreme commander, it contained many undecipherable literary terms with exhortations to complete the final effort to drive the Americans into the sea and liberate all of Korea.

Copeland and I were having lunch with another "crypt-techie" John La Forge at a small four-man table in the enlisted man's mess hall and all three of us were discussing cryptanalysis, language and the Kim Il Sung message. Cope asked our waitress if they had "muck pee" for lunch. She giggled as always and ran away. We all laughed and reflected on the menu in Kim Il Sung's message. I said it was very helpful to pick up messages in the codebook, but it was still missing many code entries. La Forge piped up that he had decrypted the same message that morning in another lower-level system.

Returning from lunch I stopped by the translation room and sure enough that message was in a pile awaiting translation. Astoundingly, a regiment to battalion message contained the complete message in a letter-for-letter simple cipher that was broken weeks before. This was a serious violation of communications security and the answer to a code breaker's dream - to encipher the same message verbatim in two different cryptographic systems. It enabled the recovery of about ninety-percent of the remaining codebook. We literally knew what the North Korean Army was having for lunch – in a way of speaking.

The North Korean 6th division was moving down the West Coast in an obvious attempt to outflank the main UN forces defending the "Pusan Perimeter". It reported its location daily by radio using a simple code. This permitted General Walker to hold off committing any of his meager forces to block the NKPA 6th until the last minute, when he threw the 27th "Wolfhounds" Regimental Combat Team at them. Colonel John “Mike” Michaelis one of the most outstanding combat officers of the perimeter defense led the 27th. The 89th Tank Battalion also made its first appearance using "General Sherman" medium tanks that were now a match for the surprised North Koreans' who were previously unbeatable in their Russian T-34's. The first contingent of U. S. Marines joined the fray and the North Korean attack was stopped.

The very nature of the Korean language rendered the code breaking relatively effortless. "Hangul" or the script used by the North Korean Army in 1950 had been standardized and in full use despite the efforts by the Japanese from 1910 until 1945 to eradicate it. The script consisted of 24 symbols - 14 consonants and 10 vowels that are combined in a very exacting manner to form pronounceable syllables. Every syllable starts with one of the consonants followed by a vowel - two symbols are sufficient to form a syllable in this manner. Vowels can be combined to form diphthongs of two vowels and rarely three. Finally, a consonant can be used to complete the syllable - uncommonly two consonants. Thus the pattern of symbols or "letters" is always one of the following: CV (consonant-vowel the most frequent formation); CVV; CVVV (rare); CVC (very frequent); CVVC; CVCC; and rarely CVVCC or CVVVCC. There are a few consonants that may be doubled at the beginning or ending of a syllable.

The frequency distribution of the symbols or "letters" in any length of text is quite marked particularly the initial and terminal consonants. The combinatorial affinity of the various symbols is extremely pronounced. This frequency of letters in any language is the bread-and-butter of successful cryptanalysis. See the Korean Language frequency distribution in the appendix.

In the simple letter substitution cryptograms that are an essential component of the entertainment section of a newspaper or puzzle magazine, the solution is usually developed by a combination of word guessing and letter frequencies. In an American newspaper the letters in the order ETAOINSHRDLU are the most numerous. Additionally a good puzzle solver would surmise the single letters "I" and "A" as well as the frequent two letter prepositions and pronouns. In the Korean script, frequency alone would produce a solution, without any knowledge of the textual context. Additionally, the sentence structure of Korean is rigid as to the sequence of subject, object (if present) and verb. Syntactically similar to Japanese, each grammatical component is indicated by a "postposition" or syllable. Furthermore, the utilitarian syllables that constitute verb endings are uniform and can readily be foreseen. East Asian languages always use a "counter" or numerative to indicate numeric quantities - similar to "panes" of glass, "head" of cattle or "rounds" of ammunition.

The above idiosyncrasies of the Korean language, combined with the repetitive nature of military communications greatly simplified the solution of encryption systems. Military terminology in messages emphasized addressee's, originator of the message, officers' ranks, unit designation (division, regiment, etc.), place names (villages, hills, rivers, roads), weapons, supplies, ammunition and most importantly of all - numerals.

Dates and times always occur in predictable formats such as:

1 0 Month 0 7 Day 1 4 Hour 3 0 Minute.

Quantities of ammunition or weapons:

2 5 Rounds 1 2 2 Mortar shells.

Military unit designations:

3 Corps 1 8 Division 2 5 Regiment 2 Battalion.

1 8 7 American Parachute Regiment.

(The U. S. Army's 187th Airborne Regimental Combat Team as actually reported as opposing a NKPA division). Detection of the numbers within a message was the primary method of cryptanalytic attack although this was coupled with the formulaic structure of combat reports, supply requests and battle orders.

One night Jack LaDove and myself were working the early evening shift with little to do as things were slow with very sparse traffic coming in. A partially decrypted message was on my desk from a North Korean coastal defense unit that described an American "Battleship" with its searchlights trained on the shore and blasting away at various targets. We openly discussed the message and I said it was probably the cruiser "Rochester", flagship of the Seventh Fleet as we were not aware of any battleships in the region. Furthermore, a boyhood pal of mine was a signalman on the "Rochester", who was a specialist in using the hand semaphore flags in communication between ships.

Jack immediately jumped-up from his desk, whipped out a handkerchief from his pocket, borrowed another, and starting wigwagging in mock semaphore and singing "Anchors Away". I did the same as others joined in. Hearing the commotion in the adjacent translators' room Captain Kim entered the decryption room, laughed and watched the show as Jack continued to tap dance around the room. The captain considered all cryptanalysis technicians slightly insane, but always enjoyed the occasional antics that broke up the somber tedium of decrypting enemy messages.

After we settled down he asked what was up. The message was pointed out to him with the comment that the location of the report was the city of Kilchu off the East Coast of North Korea. I said that the cruiser's eight-inch guns were probably leveling the nearby key railroad junction. He glanced at the message, his mood changed and tears came to his eyes as he said nothing and left the room. We all looked puzzled as a crypt-techie broke the silence with the comment that none of us were aware of - "The captain's mother still lives in North Korea". [She was later evacuated from there with thousands of other refugees when the UN forces pulled out after it had been occupied for several weeks.]

The volume of decrypted and plain text messages still overwhelmed the translators. The crypt techies were still working twelve-hour shifts, sometimes sleeping on top of desks or on a cot in the room. We never closed up the office, so all materials were left out on desks. Some newly arrived men could not adapt to using the Korean language. They attempted a time-consuming process of calligraphy in drawing the Korean syllables as they decoded a message. This not only put a heavier burden on the productive code breakers, but also caused the translators to return the message in exasperation and complain about its readability.

The officers in charge could do nothing about this situation as they themselves lacked knowledge about the Korean language as well as the current cryptography.

Their careers were now on the line as the abdicated real control and begrudgingly let the efficient enlisted men and translators run the show. The ineffective cryptographers were shunted aside, assuming duties as messengers, typists, clerks and one did nothing much else but make coffee.

An "ad hoc" system had taken over in the last month. The incoming intercepted messages were prioritized and parceled out to the most capable decoders. If a message was unbreakable it was placed on my desk. No new North Korean system went unbroken for more than 24 hours.

It appeared that the translators were on duty incessantly. Some just took catnaps on small cots set up in their office and in the conference room on the first floor. One day Major Swears told Norman Wild that he didn't want him to work too hard then asked him how many hours a day was he working. Norman irritated by the pseudo-concern and in addition to a civilian's disdain for military officers replied: "What's 24 divided by one?"

A NKPA Corps to headquarters report in Mid-August gave the disposition of a massing of several divisions poised to launch a penetration of the perimeter. This was made possible by the now virtual full recovery of the NKPA codebook. That night this information was flashed to the Eighth Army's General "Johnny" Walker who arranged his battered and meager forces accordingly and requested a heavy B-29 bombing of the area where the North Korean's were concentrated. There has since been some inter-service controversy over the effectiveness of this low-level saturation raid. However, that particular Corps radio went silent for the next few days and the offensive did not materialize as planned. The "Pusan Perimeter" held.

While concentrating on North Korean traffic the Russian side was not neglected. A major concern was still the Soviet Air Force presence in the Far East - there was a continuous search for any long-range bomber activity with its potential nuclear weapons delivery capabilities. All major Soviet military, air and army, circuits since December 1949 no longer transmitted readable messages, but we still scanned their communications. Traffic analysis placed many Russian units in Manchuria - opposite the Korean border.

We picked-up messages that were identified as coming from the Russian 3rd long-range Bomber Air Army that was based near the city of Chita in Siberia. They were broadcasting "blindly"; that is, nobody acknowledged receipt of the traffic or requested retransmission due to interference - atmospheric or manmade. The traffic was sent in standard five digit groups, but I noticed that there was a significant four-digit pattern. If the message was transcribed into four digit groupings a definite structure emerged. The first and second digits when added to the third and fourth digit always summed to 9. As follows: 2178 4257 0099 9603 and so on in a random fashion. It was obviously practice or "dummy" traffic and a report was drafted accordingly. Although, at first, there was some resistance to my presentation, it later became the first instance of Soviet fabrication of radio messages during the cold war.

The Korean front stabilized, although there were intense battles no large quantities of real estate changed hands. In Tokyo, more translators and cryptanalytic technicians were arriving bringing the staff to over 30 people. Some of our former schoolmates from ASA School at Carlisle Barracks, as well as transferees from ASA units in Europe, were quickly brought up to speed on the Korean language and NKPA cryptography. Everyone, regardless of rank, was assigned to rotating shifts to give full and timely coverage to processing North Korean communications. The translators both military and civilian were still putting in exhausting hours.

In the early hours of September 15th 1950, I was working the midnight to eight AM shift, but there was virtually nothing intercepted on the NKPA networks that night. Since there was not much to work on, I was asleep at my desk with my head resting on my right arm in a cast stretched across the desk. I had fractured my radius in a motor scooter accident two weeks before.

Lt. Elinora M. Toft, Women's Army Corps, the school-marmish officer on duty that night came over to my desk and shook me awake. "John - John you'll have to wake up. There are a lot of people downstairs". I jumped up and said "Yes, yes - has anything come in yet?" She replied "No, nothing", then turned to several other enlisted men "Look alive, important things are happening" as she left the room.

Operation "Chromite", the Inchon Landing was underway. The small two story white concrete building on a former Japanese Imperial Army Base in Northern Tokyo was ablaze in lights at four o'clock in the morning, with intelligence officers anxiously awaiting any enemy reaction to the Allied attack. There were many rumors going around; Five allied destroyers were sunk in Inchon's "Flying Fish" channel or that the North Koreans were unleashing over 200 aircraft they had hidden in caves. None of this happened.

I went through the age-old ritual of spreading books and papers about the desk to look busy. There were no new codes to break. The North Korean Peoples Army (NKPA) had maintained an ominous and troubling radio silence for two days. I went to my triple-locked file cabinet and dug out some Soviet Air Force traffic that I had been working on recently and proceeded to study it.

After a while, Lt. Toft returned with some canary yellow intercepts and came over to my desk. "These just came in, it's a new network, we haven't heard it before" she said as she laid them on my desk. I looked at several pages of four digit groups that looked vaguely familiar. I said "Thank you" as she looked over my shoulder for a moment then returned to her desk.

It was a syllabic substitution system similar to one I had broken two months ago - the pre-war NKPA traffic. It took about a half-hour to reduce the specific key. I turned and asked Lt. Toft "Who is translating this morning? This stuff is just about ready". She left the room and returned with Captain Youn P. Kim, who pulled up a chair and sat down next to me.

The Pyongyang-born WWII veteran Captain and myself had a developed a close relationship in the past two months. There was no military formality. We frequently, on a day-to-day basis, consulted with each other on Korean terminology or cryptographic nuances. Although he lacked the academic credentials of some of his civilian colleague translators, he had an uncanny military knack of winnowing out the most important military messages. He was without a doubt the most prolific and valuable translator.

I pointed to the first message and said "I'm not sure about this number, it's either a 6 or 7. Evidently, the message is from the 26th or 27th some-kind-of Brigade, what do you make of it?" The Captain looked-up at me, startled. "It is the Inchon situation report from a unit of the 27th coastal-defense brigade. The marines have taken Wolmi-do Island in Inchon harbor". I made several corrections to the Korean text as he looked on and made a few suggestions. He then said "I'll take this one, get the rest to me as fast as you can".

The first message was translated and flashed to General MacArthur on board the command ship Mt. McKinley, off the West Coast of Korea. It was reported that the General was pleased. Subsequent messages in this system indicated that the 27th Coastal Defense Brigade was headquartered in the Munsan area. It directed units of the 17th and 18th Divisions, deployed west of Han River, to counter-attack the Inchon beachhead. Two columns of six Russian T-34 tanks each, accompanied by infantry, were ordered to ambush the advancing first marine division at two specific locations.

On September 16th, the first column was found three miles east of Inchon and attacked by two flights of "Corsair" aircraft from the aircraft carrier Sicily. One American plane was shot down killing the marine pilot. A follow-up assault by combined infantry and "Pershing" tanks completed the destruction of the column. In the early morning of the 17th the 5th Marines set up an ambush of their own and annihilated the second column killing over 200 North Koreans. The Inchon landing was secured.

In early October Captain Kim, Lieutenant Chun and PFC Dick Copeland were dispatched to Korea to link up with the 60th Signal Service Company to set up an ASAPAC advanced decoding and translation unit. Kim had an opportunity to view the destroyed Russian T-34 tanks and reported back the scene to us in Tokyo.

Several days later the U. S. Marines reciprocated the Army's intelligence contribution to their efforts. The first hard-copy confirmation of our code-breaking efforts arrived. The NKPA codebook had been captured, supposedly by the marines as they overran the 18th NKPA Division's command post. Major Swears came into the office looking for me. I was downstairs in the latrine, so codebook in hand, he encountered me as I was zipping up and walking away from a urinal. "The marines picked this up this morning" he said as he handed it to me. It was flown from recently re-taken Kimpo airfield to Tokyo. The big numerals "001" were printed on the cover of a roughly 14 inch by 8 inch thin book. I glanced through it and saw we were right on target as far as our code recoveries were concerned, with only a few synonymous variations. The Major stepped up to a urinal as I replied "Too bad, they stopped using it two days ago, but it will sure confirm a lot of our assumptions, thanks". It was a strange location to discuss one of the significant intelligence coups of the Korean War.

I always wanted to meet up with and buy a drink for the marine or marines responsible for this. They realized the codebook's value, and rather than keep it as a souvenir, which was frequently the case, it was speedily forwarded to the right headquarters.

Some large North Korean units had panicked and were transmitting in plain text again. A new "Defense Command" was established to control the fighting in the West and the defense of Seoul. The "front-line HQ" was directing the NKPA withdrawal in the East. They talked about heading North through the Mountains as best they could. Fortunately, when the lines stabilized the NKPA resumed using the codebook and numerous variations throughout the first year of the war. It proved to be a valuable intelligence asset.

In late September I asked Dugan to see if any more of the pre-war messages might still be over in the Traffic Analysis building. The intercepts that I previously isolated only ran through early May. Since the same type system was used by the Inchon defense forces I was concerned that there may be similar systems in store for us as we moved north and encountered defensive formations. He returned later that day with a bunch of traffic that ran right up to June 22nd. I scanned through them and found no difference in the encryption system and filed it in my locked cabinet with the rest of the traffic that was intercepted prior to June 25th.---

---

Initial Consonant------>

ㄱ ㄴ ㄷ ㄹ ㅁ ㅂ ㅅ ㅇ ㅈ ㅊ ㅋ ㅌ ㅍ ㅎ ㄲ ㄸ ㅃ ㅆ ㅉ

1 2 3 4 5 6 7 8 9 01 02 03 04 05 06 07 08 09 00

Vowels----------------->

ㅏ ㅑ ㅓ ㅕ ㅗ ㅛ ㅜ ㅠ ㅡ ㅣ ㅐ ㅔ ㅖ ㅘ ㅝ ㅟ

1 2 3 4 5 6 7 8 91 92 93 94 95 96 97 98 99

Terminal Consonant (if present else 0 or 00)----->

ㄱ ㄴ ㄹ ㅁ ㅂ ㅅ ㅇ ㅍ ㅎ ㄶ ㄺ ㅄ ㅆ

1 2 3 4 5 6 7 8 91 92 93 94 95 96 97 98 99

Cryptographic System used by the North Korean Peoples Army prior to June 25th 1950. A similar system was used by the Coastal Defense Brigade opposing the Inchon invasion. The methodology is unique to the Korean Language in which all syllables are constructed with an initial consonant followed by a vowel or vowels. A final consonant or consonants may be added. The numeric values were substituted for the Korean symbols. Each syllable was transmitted as a four-digit group zeroes filling out the group if the syllable encryption was less than four. Some diphthongs and final consonants were not encountered therefore no assumption was made as to the numeric value.

Chapter V

October November December 1950

Radio comments heard on UN voice networks:

"Many, many Chineezu come"

"Holy shit, there's a million of them"

"We're pullin` a "Hank Snow" - we're movin' on"-

六. 情报与军事指挥

Intelligence and Command

侦 察 reconnaissance
侦察机构 reconnaissance agency
侦察部队 reconnaissance troops
侦察人员 reconnaissance personnel
侦 察 员 reconnaissance scout
侦察工具 reconnaissance implements
侦 察 车 recnnaissance car
侦察坦克 reconnaissance tank
侦 察 台 reconnaissance station
侦察电视 reconnaissance television
侦察对象 reconnaissance object
侦察活动 reconnaissance activity
侦察情报 reconnaissance intelligence
敌情资料 reconnaissance data
特种侦察 special reconnaissance
谍报侦察 espionage reconnaissance
敌情侦察 reconnaissance of enemy's situation
地形侦察 topographical reconnaissance

— 40 —

社情侦察 reconnaissance of social situation
地面侦察 ground reconnaissance
作战侦察 operational reconnaissance
战略侦察 strategic reconnaissance
战术侦察 tactical reconnaissance
战场侦察 reconnaissance of battlefield
威力侦察 reconnaissance in force
火力侦察 reconnaissance by fire
水面侦察 surface reconnaissance
水道侦察 hydrographic reconnaissance
海上侦察 marine reconnaissance
空中侦察 air reconnaissance
卫星侦察 reconnaissance by satellite
航天侦察 spaceflight reconnaissance
联合侦察 joint reconnaissance
技术侦察 technical reconnaissance
电子侦察 electronic reconnaissance
放射性侦察 rediation reconnaissance
无线电技术侦察 reconnaissance of radio technique
雷达侦察 radar reconnaissance
无线电侦听 radio interception
侦 听 台 intercept station
无线电侦听台 radio interception station
监 听 moritoring

— 41 —

--- Pinyin Chinese-English Military Dictionary showing the depth of intelligence awareness --

After the success of the Inchon landing and the subsequent 8th Army drive into North Korea, American overconfidence returned.

Although the subject of Chinese forces taking part in the Korean conflict was discussed there was no assigned intercept mission to monitor their armies' communications within ASAPAC's area - the Japanese islands or Korea. The newly formed U. S. Air Force Security Service had an intercept unit at Johnson Air Force base just outside Tokyo. We received nothing from them at this time, the two dozen Army intercept operators on loan to the Air Force having returned to ASAPAC in Tokyo.

The situation was compounded by a major lapse of communications intelligence logistics. It was necessary to bring a mobile ASA unit to give close support to Eighth United States Army in Korea (designated as EUSAK). There were two ASA mobile radio intercept units available in the continental states, the 53rd Signal Service Company (SSC) at Vint Hill Farms, Virginia and the 60th Signal Service Company located at Fort Lewis, Washington.

The mobile segment of the 53rd had recently returned from Army maneuvers in North Carolina, while the permanent party remained at Vint Hill Farms Station for intercept duties, primarily diplomatic traffic from the Washington D. C. area.

In early August the 60th SSC was alerted for shipment to Korea. It shut down operations and everything transportable was packed and the unit awaited shipment orders. Unfortunately, one mission of the 60th was to monitor Chinese Army communications. Although some intercept operators were transferred to Two Rock Ranch Station in Petaluma, California there would be a Chinese Army radio intelligence hiatus from August until late October. There were no cryptanalytic personnel with the 60th, but the day before shipping out of Ft. Lewis they were joined by enlisted code breakers from the 53rd, including Jim McCloy and Joe Chaney our classmates from the ASA school at Carlisle Barracks.

On October 9th, 1950, the Army Security Agency's 60th Signal Service Company after departing from Seattle, and after a stop at San Francisco, debarked at Pusan, Korea with all their mobile equipment. Translators Captain Youn P. Kim, Lt. Richard Chun and cryptanalytic technician PFC Dick Copeland were detached from ASAPAC Tokyo and shipped over to Korea by LST (Landing Ship Tank) from Sasebo, Japan to join them. They were to set up an advanced decryption and translation team to directly service 8th Army Headquarters with NKPA intercepts.

The about 200 man unit split into several parts, with a base unit outside of Seoul, a small detachment with EUSAK-advance which eventually encamped near a "liberated" brewery in Pyongyang, and a scattering of radio direction-finding sights. The intercept operators of the 60th were adept at Chinese Army communications procedure, but were unfamiliar with North Korean. The two methodologies were as different as night and day, including "cut-numbers", so it took the ditty-boppers (Military Occupation Specialty; Radio Intercept Operator - MOS 799) some time to get accustomed to North Korean practices.

U. S. Military commanders in Washington, Tokyo and Korea became overly dependent upon communications intelligence, particularly the flow of North Korean message translations from our cryptanalytic effort in Tokyo. Every encrypted North Korean message to date was readable. Analogous to narcotic dependency, the absence of any Chinese messages, caused them to assume there was no movement underway.

To achieve the element of surprise in any modern military operation it is decreed that complete radio silence should be in effect. The Chinese Peoples Volunteer Army performed this to perfection. Before crossing the Yalu River all radios were confiscated. It was a prudent yet unnecessary effort as there were no ears tuned in to their radio signals. If there had been, the sudden absence of traffic would have been significant.

On October 25th we received a message from General MacArthur's Headquarters - "GENERAL WILLOUGHBY EXPECTS CHINESE FORCES TO CROSS YALU RIVER TONIGHT. REQUEST YOUR AGENCY BE ON ALERT". The message was placed on Lt. Julia Chapman's desk that she maintained in the Cryptanalysis room. No action was taken as she was at a cocktail party in downtown Tokyo. As yet there were no intercept positions dedicated to Chinese networks.

Within the next few weeks several Chinese prisoners were captured, some in North Korean uniforms. POW interrogation reports stated that the 40th Chinese Peoples Army was identified along with the 117th, 119th and 120th divisions. A Chinese "Army" is equivalent in command structure to a U. S. "Corps". Although the Chinese "Volunteers" were authorized radios down to the regimental level, they were either confiscated or ordered to maintain total radio silence. They also had elaborate subterfuges to use in case of capture to falsify the identity of their units. Some prisoners stated that they crossed the Yalu River from Manchuria on the 16th of October. Newspaper reports claimed there were over 20,000 Chinese soldiers already in Korea.

November 2nd was the date of the "Official" recognition that the Chinese had jumped in with both feet. Captain Ligon set up a belated Chinese cryptanalytic team with Jack LaDove in charge. This was rather odd as he was a Private, First Class (PFC) and the team included Captain Sid Haken and several sergeants. Secondly, there was very little traffic available, only random intercepts from search missions in Japan. For wearing unpolished officer's brass and not wearing a belt Captain Ligon chastised one reluctant recently activated reserve second Lieutenant assigned to the team.

The first thing Jack asked for was a copy of the Chinese Telegraphic Code (CTC) also known as the "Ming" codebook. This was a four-digit code, with 10,000 entries of Chinese characters - a readily available commercial document that was around since the 1920's. It permitted the transmission of the numeric equivalent of Chinese ideographs by radio or telegraphic landlines. Ligon said he would see about getting a copy. When I said that there was a copy floating around in translation as well as the Traffic Analysis section he just glared.

We were unaware of a similar Chinese team at Arlington Hall, as no correspondence took place. The cryptanalytic and translation efforts seemed to be all located in Tokyo, although there were intercept facilities in the Philippines, Hawaii and California. No Chinese Army traffic was forwarded to Tokyo from these installations. Again, a logistics blunder.

Fortunately the North Korean Army continued to transmit considerable traffic, although they were in the process of reorganizing. Stragglers that were cut off by the Inchon landing were now regrouping and new units were being formed. The Eighth Army was driving into North Korea, but the NKPA was still offering resistance.

On November 1st the "Turbina" or Russian jet aircraft made its debut. The MIG-15 was now sighted over North Korea. At first the MIG's left in a hurry when challenged, but soon started to attack the B-29 formations as well as reconnaissance aircraft. The battle for air supremacy was starting. "Recon" flights were cut back at a very critical time.

When most of the fighting took place in South Korea, there was Republic of Korea agents that remained behind the lines and were able to obtain and transmit valuable intelligence information. Now in the North no such apparatus existed. As far as HUMINT (Human intelligence) was concerned we were "flying blind" in North Korea, with no agents on the ground.

There was an attempt to alleviate this situation. Early one evening in the middle of the November, Sgt. Frank Dugan was the night NCO on duty at "ASAPAC's - Tokyo Black Chamber". He was scanning some unfamiliar coded messages that were intercepted on a heretofore-unidentified North Korean network, when he received a phone call from General Willoughby's office. Dugan knew the Sergeant calling and speaking over the open, unsecured telephone asked if there was anything unusual that ASAPAC picked-up this evening. Dugan replied that he wasn't sure. The G-2 Sergeant said "The General has something big going on tonight and would appreciate anything that we might come up with". Dugan replied "We'll get right on it, but it may take some time". The caller said, "OK, thanks" and hung up.

Sgt. Dugan dialed the motor pool and ordered a Jeep and driver at once. He got up from his desk, put on his "Eisenhower" jacket and asked the two other men in the room "Anybody know where Milmore was headed tonight?" LaForge answered "Try the Iroha". "Good" he said as he went to a safe and removed and strapped on the holstered standard .45 caliber pistol. "If anybody asks, I went looking for John". PFC LaForge asked, "What are you going to do, shoot him?" Dugan laughed as he picked up three messages, folded them neatly and put them in the breast pocket of his jacket. "No I'm carrying classified material, you know the rules" he replied as he left the office.

The I-ro-ha Bar was a larger than usual Japanese restaurant. Staffed by young semi-pretty girls who tried to indulge the off duty GI's from the local base. There were about 10 soldiers and half-dozen girls inside when the jeep screeched to a halt outside. "MP's, MP's" the girls screamed with a look of mock terror on their faces.

Everybody laughed, since the onset of the Korean War Military Police were never around this part of northern Tokyo. Many of them had gone to Korea as combat MP's and some were never coming back.

Dugan slid the door open and stepped in. He looked down the Bar, but was disappointed. "Anybody seen Milmore" he asked in an official tone. "Yea, he's in the side room, but he may be busy" said Cpl. Kraus with an evil leer.

Dugan peered into the tatami (straw mat) floored room and motioned to me to come over. As he took out the three canary yellow messages he said, "I think this is important. You'd better come back to the section". I glanced at the material and laughingly replied "What are you doing with this stuff here? Isn't it classified?" I handed back the messages and put my boots on.

As we returned to base in the jeep Dugan filled me in on the request from downtown. I said keep the jeep available. Back at the office there were several more messages, with the normal four digit numeric groups badly split and an intercept operator's comment "This guy sounds like he's sending with his left foot".

The system was a simple two-digit mono-alphabetic substitution with four variant cipher alphabets. Some messages had the cipher equivalents in rotational order; others randomly as was the probable intention and some used only the first column of numerals from 00 to 25. The Korean "Onmun" or Han Gul "alphabet" sequence with the Western alphabet equivalents.

Plain	Variant cipher equivalent				
K	00	25	50	75	00 Through 13 are the consonants with approximate pronounceable equivalent/
N	01	26	51	76	
T	02	27	52	77	
L	03	28	53	78	
M	04	29	54	79	
P	05	30	55	80	
S	06	31	56	81	
Ng	07	32	57	82	Not initially voiced
J	08	33	58	83	
Ch	09	34	59	84	09 through 12 are soft (aspirated) consonants
Kh	10	35	60	85	
Th	11	36	61	86	
Ph	12	37	62	87	
H	13	38	63	88	
A	14	39	64	89	14 through 23 are vowels
YA	15	40	65	90	
U	16	41	66	91	
YU	17	42	67	92	
O	18	43	68	93	
YO	19	44	69	94	
OO	20	45	70	95	
YOO	21	46	71	96	
EU	22	47	72	97	
I	23	48	73	98	
Period	24	49	74	99	Punctuation/ End of sentence-

Letter	Cipher Equivalent			
ㄱ	01	26	51	76
ㄴ	02	27	52	77
ㄷ	03	28	53	78
ㄹ	04	29	54	79
ㅁ	05	30	55	80
ㅂ	06	31	56	81
ㅅ	07	32	57	82
ㅇ	08	33	58	83
ㅈ	09	34	59	84
ㅊ	10	35	60	85
ㅋ	11	36	61	86
ㅌ	12	37	62	87
ㅍ	13	38	63	88
ㅎ	14	39	64	89
ㅏ	15	40	65	90
ㅑ	16	41	66	91
ㅓ	17	42	67	92
ㅕ	18	43	68	93
ㅗ	19	44	69	94
ㅛ	20	45	70	95
ㅜ	21	46	71	96
ㅠ	22	47	72	97
ㅡ	23	48	73	98
ㅣ	24	49	74	99
period.	25	50	75	00

Same system in Korean.

It was a North Korean police or constabulary network, previously not intercepted. It was alive with reports of single parachutists dropping at different locations. One jumper turned himself in to the local police as soon as he landed. He was a double agent. Before leaping from the aircraft he hurled a hand-grenade inside the C-47 transport. The aircraft caught fire and crashed and the U. S. Army Sergeant jumpmaster survived, was captured and imprisoned for the rest of the war.

The large-scale espionage operation was compromised. The constabulary network alerted all other units as to the location of the other drops. Communications contained information on the captured agents including names, missions and inventory of their equipment.

The messages were quickly translated and flashed to Willoughby's office. Further drops planned for that night were canceled; some aircraft were already airborne while others were on runways ready to take off. I typed up the solution for transmittal to the ASA unit in Korea and to Arlington Hall, took the jeep and was back at the I-Ro-Ha bar by nine o'clock. They had kept my unfinished bottle of beer in the refrigerator.

North Korean Army and Air Force traffic volume started to increase as the resistance to Eighth Army's advances stiffened. The Chinese attacked, then withdrew. The intelligence picture was muddled. There still were no intercept positions assigned to intercept Chinese Army traffic. The prewar North Korean Peoples Army traffic was still sitting in my file cabinet - decrypted, yet not translated. It would have provided valuable data on the bases in the vastness of North Korea - that permitted the NKPA to regroup, re-arm and hide the Chinese forces waiting to pounce.

That they did, in a coordinated NKPA and massive Chinese assault. On November 28th a North

Korean Air Force message was picked up in their simple cipher system - the first system I broke back in June. They stated their intention to attack the U. S. Air Force based at the recently captured Pyongyang airport. Dick Copeland in Korea decrypted it and the 60th Signal Service Company forwarded the translation, but it was ignored at Fifth Air Force Headquarters. This was probably because they assumed they had complete air superiority. Six F-51 Mustangs were destroyed on the ground and there was one fatality. "Bed Check Charlie" had made his first kill.

Back in October General MacArthur directed the Tenth (X) Corps to embark on another amphibious landing on the Northeast coast of North Korea. The newly arrived 3rd Division joined the other divisions of the X Corps - the First Marine and the 7th Infantry.

The U. S. Marines were delayed in their landing at Wonsan in North Korea by mines in Wonsan harbor - unknown to American intelligence. This was unfortunate, as Bob Hope was waiting to entertain them - having recently arrived by air in an area liberated by a South Korean division that raced up the East Coast. The Seventh Division debarked further north along the coast at Iwon and then its 17th regiment immediately drove to Hyesanjin on the Yalu River.

The Marines finally got to see Bob Hope at Wonsan, then moved into North Korea on each side of the Chosin reservoir. The Tenth Corps, under the command of General Almond, General MacArthur's chief of staff, then committed one of the biggest blunders in military history. Without any communications intelligence or aerial observation of Chinese movements and disregarding reports of captured Chinese prisoners, the tenth corps' Marines and Seventh Infantry Division were thinly spread out across Northeast Korea. The Chinese attacked and then withdrew. The X corps countered by moving a marine regiment from East of the Chosin reservoir to the West and filling the void with two battalions of the Seventh division from two separate regiments. Three Chinese Armies surrounded the reservoir and attacked, wiping out the two-army battalions and forcing the Marines to fight their way out.

The Chinese forces were able to move swiftly through pre-established bases, guided by North Korea Army forces that assisted in the attack with tanks and armored vehicles. They did not need radio communication. The Americans, who rely heavily on communications, were unable to establish contact between the Army and Marines, as well as between the two disjointed battalions and supporting tanks and artillery.

It was an intelligence and command disaster. The same thing was happening with the Eighth Army North of Pyongyang in the Western part of North Korea. Over extended and over reliant on communications intelligence - which wasn't there - General Johnny Walkers Army was in full retreat.

When the first G-3 (operations) situation report map, that indicated Chinese units, was received in the cryptanalysis section of ASAPAC several of us including some officers were passing it around and discussing it. Six Chinese armies surrounded the first marine division. I said they'd never make it out. I was subsequently proven wrong. I then asked where was the 60th Signal Service Company, our ASA unit in North Korea. Two officers looked at each other and quickly left the room.

It appears that no order was given to withdraw the 60th before the Chinese overran them. Dick Copeland later reported they had to sidetrack the retreating Second Division to let the 60th drive by. That was after the commander of all ASA units in Korea, a ludicrous Major Degenhardt had ordered them to keep one bullet and prepare to take their own lives before being captured, as he climbed aboard his small aircraft and flew South. Jim McCloy told Copeland that he would keep two bullets, one in case Degenhardt returned. [Degenhardt was later relieved of his command by General Van Fleet in a covered over scandal. There were many salacious rumors concerning this event none worth mentioning. He was drummed out of the Army Security Agency.]

The Chinese People's Volunteer Army, in conjunction with a surprisingly rejuvenated North Korean People's Army were chasing the Tenth Corps and the Eighth United States Army in the longest retreat ever suffered by American forces.

General Lin Piao, commanding about 200,000 men, had the radio communication facilities, which were the equivalent of an American battalion commander - one radio truck. He rarely used it and even more rarely did we intercept any messages, having no experience factor on transmission schedules or frequencies used. His army only moved at night, blanking out our air observation - the intelligence picture on the Chinese Armies' intent and capabilities was pure speculation.

Providentially, the North Koreans continued to use their radios. They frequently screened movements of Chinese units or replaced them when in a defensive mode. The main NKPA network continued to use a 500 group additive page. However, they renumbered their basic "001" tactical codebook. We had completely recovered this code, with confirmation from a captured copy.

A new wrinkle was introduced. They reconstructed this codebook to make it a two-part code. They probably did this by pasting numeric strips down the side of the codebook over the original code-number entries, which was standard Russian practice. They similarly had to have added a conversion table for decoding purposes. Here is an example of a two-part code from the manual on basic cryptography written in 1935.

The following brief extracts from typical one-part and two-part codes will serve to illustrate the difference between them:

One-part code.		Two-part code.			
		Encoding Section		Decoding Section	
ABABD	A	GAJVY	A	ABABD	Obstructed
ABACF	Abaft	TOGTY	Abaft	ABACF	Term
ABAHK	Abandon	FEHIL	Abandon	ABAHK	Zero
ABAJL	.... it	BAYLT	.... it	ABAJL	If it has not
ABALN	Abandoned	ZYZYZ	Abandoned	ABALN	To be sent by
ABAMP	.... by	NYSYZ	.... by	ABAMP	Acceding
ABAWZ	Abandoning	IFWUZ	Abandoning	ABAWZ	Building
ABBAD	Abandonment	RUMGO	Abandonment	ABBAD	Do not attempt
....		....		....	
ZYZYZ	Zero	ABAHK	Zero	ZYZYZ	Abandoned

75. Purposes of the two-part type of code.—*a*. The two-part code is a comparatively recent development in code systems. Its purposes are two-fold: (1) Greater secrecy, and (2) greater accuracy. These two features will now be explained.

This type of code does not have the alphabetized plain text equivalents in a matched numeric or alphabetic sequence. It becomes slightly more difficult to use, but infinitely more laborious to break. Luckily, their method of randomization, to re-number the codebook, had patterns that I freely exploited. We were never blacked-out, although there were delays and for a time incomplete translations.

In mid-December Major Swears called me down to his office and asked me "what kind of trouble was I into lately". He then laughed and handed me a GHQ Certificate of Achievement signed by Colonel Greiner (see appendix). In general the certificate referred to activities from the onset of hostilities, but Swears said it was for preserving General Willoughby's aborted airdrop of agents a few weeks ago.

I took the certificate back upstairs and passed it around the office. Jack LaDove held it up saying, "This looks just like an Ohio State Liquor License. After the war you could open a saloon in Cleveland with it".

Everybody laughed except Ligon who glared at him and hissed "I wouldn't belittle that if I were you, LaDove". There was no love lost between the two.

Sporadic Chinese traffic was now coming in. Jack, who was heading-up a Chinese cryptanalysis group never received a copy of the Chinese Telegraphic Codebook. Needless to say, there was very little productivity from codebreaking of Chinese Army communications. Jack applied for a transfer to the post engineers, as there was an opening for a draftsman - his civilian specialty. He cited "being engaged in a fruitless endeavor" in his request for transfer.

A month later on January 21st, while involved with the move of the expanding decoding section to the ground floor of the Headquarters building, Jack found a copy of the Chinese Telegraphic Code, stamped Top Secret, wedged in the rear portion of the CH-76 safe. He confronted Captain Ligon with it, who turned crimson and stammered "sometimes it helps to move" then added "I looked it over and there's not much in it". The next day Jack received his transfer out of the code-breaking section to S-4 (logistics Section). He was furious, but did not know who to report it to - this obvious sabotage or gross negligence involving the Chinese cryptanalytic effort.

---The author, John LaForge, Frank Dugan and Milton Pagel – ASAPAC cryptanalysis Technicians – Tokyo Christmas 1950.

Below Captain Richard Ligon and First lieutenant Elinora Toft at the same party.---

Chapter VI

January, February, March and April 1951
- The One That Got Away -
- Boustrophedonic Fibonacci -
- "Pearl Harbor" Message -
- A trip to Chitose, Hokkaido ---

Bill "Blinky" O'Brien, John Milmore and Richard Copeland
Tokyo, February 1951 - GHQ Enlisted Men's Club.

On the first day of January 1951 the reconstructed and re-equipped North Korean Peoples Army instituted a new element in their organization - a political security officer was assigned to each major military unit. In effect he was a spy, to ferret out disloyalty, and was authorized to communicate in his own cipher directly with Internal Security Headquarters in PyongYang. Not only was he an internal spy, he used a classic Soviet espionage encryption system that has long stymied cryptanalysts.

These political security officers, or "commissars" as they were dubbed, did not generate much traffic. The

Chinese Communist Forces and the NKPA had launched an offensive on New Years Eve - objective Seoul. Intelligence (G-2) expressed little interest in political messages, as the decryption of the readable tactical messages had a higher priority. Evidently somebody was interested. In the book the "Puzzle Palace" (see bibliography) mention is made of evidence in the 1954 espionage trial of Joseph Sidney Petersen Jr. He had obtained a Top Secret traffic analysis known as A.F.S.A. 230763; KC037 entitled "Routing of North Korean Political Security Traffic... dated February 20, 1951". David Kahn's "The Code Breakers" also cites this trial and elsewhere in his excellent book gives details of the generic Russian cipher system that their agents employ.

The method was a simple one and two digit numeric substitution system that was then subject to transposition. Sometimes this is referred to by civilian puzzle solvers as a "straddling checkerboard", already employed by the North Korean forces, - denoted by the Russians as "monome-dinome". The generic solution of transposition requires extensive trial and error efforts, especially if "double transposition" is involved.

A simplistic sample using the American alphabet will illustrate the basic Soviet espionage coding system in use since the Spanish Civil War in the 1930`s. The normal alphabet is inscribed within the "straddling checkerboard". The first eight letters are equal to the single digits 3 through 0, the remaining are represented by a two-digit number beginning with the digit 1 or 2.

____STRADDLING CHECKERBOARD____

____1 2 3 4 5 6 7 8 9 0
___A B C D E F G H
1 I J K L M N O P Q R
2 S T U V W X Y Z . /

Plain : N O W I S T H E T I M E F O R A L
Cipher: 16 17 25 11 21 22 0 7 22 11 15 7 8 17 10 3 14

L G O O D M E N T O C O M E T O T H E I
14 9 17 17 6 15 7 16 22 17 5 17 15 7 22 17 22 0 7 11

A I D O F T H E I R P A R T Y .
3 11 6 22 8 17 0 7 11 10 18 3 10 22 17 29

The numeric cipher text is then inscribed into a ten-column rectangle. The last row is padded with nines to complete the rectangle. The digits of the cipher text are removed from the first rectangle in key headed column sequence from 1 to 0 and written into the second rectangle row by row. Finally, the digits are again removed in key column fashion from the second rectangle and the message is written into five digit groups for subsequent transmission.

Rectangle One	Rectangle Two
Key 8 5 2 7 3 6 4 9 0 1	Key 4 1 8 0 2 9 3 7 5 6
1 6 1 7 2 5 1 1 2 1	1 5 1 7 1 7 0 0 9 1
2 2 0 7 2 2 1 1 1 5	0 1 1 2 2 1 1 1 2 2
7 8 1 7 1 0 3 1 4 1	1 1 1 1 1 0 2 1 1 3
4 9 1 7 1 7 6 1 5 7	6 5 2 8 8 9 6 2 8 9
1 6 2 2 1 7 5 1 7 1	6 7 1 1 2 5 2 0 7 7
5 7 2 2 1 7 2 2 0 7	7 7 1 9 7 7 7 7 2 2
3 1 1 6 1 7 8 2 2 0	1 1 1 1 2 7 4 1 5 3
7 1 1 1 0 1 8 3 1 0	7 2 1 1 1 1 1 2 2 3
2 2 1 7 2 9 9 9 9 9	9 2 1 4 5 7 0 2 1 9

Final cipher text in five-digit groups:

51157 71221 21827 21501 26274 10101 66717 99218
72521 12397 23390 11207 12211 12111 11710 95771
77218 19114

The distorted frequency distribution of the ten digits from the 90-digit message is tabulated below. One would expect a count of roughly 9 for each of the ten digits in a random sample of this size. Any message encrypted in this system, regardless of the transposition key, would have the same relative digit frequencies.

Digit		1	2	3	4	5	6	7	8	9	0	
Frequency	=	31	17	3	2	5	3	14	3	6	6	= 90

In actual practice the single digit letter equivalents would be the most frequent letters - A E I O N R S T, different of course for Russian or whatever language was employed. This would somewhat suppress the distortion of the digit frequency distribution and lead to another use of the "straddling checkerboard" or "monome-dinome" encryption system. Instead of transposing the ciphered digits an "additive" key is generated from the text of a book, such as a widely distributed novel. The additive is then applied to the cipher text and if the generated additive is judiciously used the security of the message would approach that of the so-called "one time pad" or single usage key. Unbreakable.

It is frustrating to have a demonstrable hypothesis concerning an encryption system, yet unable to prove it with the limited resources available. The punched-card IBM 405 tabulating equipment designed in 1938 at my disposal in Tokyo was useless, rudimentary computers were available to the Armed Forces Security Agency (AFSA) in the Washington, D. C. area. There were the two programmable ENIACs, as well as other specialized decryption equipment known as Rapid Analytic Machinery (RAM). Some gained fame during World War II, including "BRUTE FORCE" and "BOMBE", in attacking the German "ENIGMA" traffic and other encryption systems using rotor machines. Furthermore, the U. S. Navy's COMINT facility known as CSAW (Communications Supplementary Activities, Washington) had just taken delivery of the first programmable magnetic drum computer "ATLAS" in December 1950. It had an advanced at the time computer instruction repertoire as well as over 49,000 bytes of storage. I am quite confident that this machine if properly programmed could have readily broken the North Korean Political Security messages. At the time it was probably employed in attacking similar Russian systems in the VENONA project.

It is doubly frustrating when the responsible cryptanalysis officer doesn't have a clue to what you are talking about or doesn't want to know. I typed up a preliminary analysis of the traffic, indicating that the single digit frequencies were markedly distorted, consistent between messages. The digit six was always predominant. I submitted it to Capt. Ligon with a suggestion that he forward it to AFSA at Arlington Hall, where they had the resources and the automatic equipment to attack the system. Nothing was ever sent and the system remained unbroken. All North Korean and Chinese cryptanalytic activity remained in Tokyo.

Dick Copeland returned from temporary duty with the 60th SSC in Korea. He regaled us with war stories including the almost capture of the 60th by the Chinese when they were never given the order to move out. The second infantry division was pulled off the road to permit the 60th to run by during the "Big Bug Out". Cope went over the new comical vernacular that developed that was part Korean, part Japanese and part GI American as typified with the Armed Forces Radio boasting a program entitled "Music Hava Yes".

Although the military situation in Korea was still critical, GHQ and ASAPAC in Tokyo was back to the occupation business-as-usual mode of operation. Minimal shift work, a skeleton crew of decipherers and translators on duty at night, and a five day work week with time off for athletics. Civilian Norman Wild the noted East Asian language scholar went back to Washington as the major translation effort shifted to the 60th in Korea.

The small South Korean Radio Intelligence unit known as ROKM or “Kim’s Group” was still performing well and the entire crew was recommended for promotion. Republic of Korea Naval Lieutenant

Commander Kim Se Won in command, with four more officers, 17 enlisted men and ten civilians mostly translators. They were on General Willoughby's "special contingency fund" payroll. They intercepted mostly plain text traffic as their radio intercept operators were naturally fluent in native Korean. Sensitive technical intelligence information such as cryptanalytic solutions from the Americans was forbidden to them. However, I was aware of one overly inquisitive translator who was slipping "Kim's Group" TOP SECRET data.

The intelligence estimate of Chinese forces in Korea varied from 150,000 up to 200,000. In actuality it was over 300,000 men, that grew to over a half-million before they departed. Sporadic Chinese traffic was now coming in and there were some translations, mostly Chinese Air Force messages in re-encrypted Chinese Telegraphic Code. This was after a very feeble start that was sabotaged by Captain Richard Ligon that caused Jack LaDove to transfer out in disgust.

For a long time Jack, Cope and myself were unable to decide if Ligon was merely incompetent, a bureaucratic martinet or actually a "mole" deliberately trying to undermine the communications intelligence effort. This suspicion spread to others, including high-ranking officers.

By February 1951, with all armies taking a breathing spell along stabilized lines, the NKPA developed their cryptography more systematically. They would change their 500 group additive page about every four weeks and repaginate their basic "001" codebook of 999 entries about every six or seven weeks. They were careful not to put both changes into effect at the same time. Any time a new encryption system was ordered it entailed much confusion and requests for retransmission's and clarification.

The new additive pages were generated from two strips of 10 three-digit groups, where the groups from strip one were added to the groups from strip two to produce the third line of additive. Then strip two was added to strip three to yield the next strip or line four. This was continued until a full 500-group page of 50 lines was completed. This is a variation of the common arithmetic series known as the Fibonacci sequence found in most High School mathematics textbooks. That is: A + B = C, B + C = D, C + D = E.... and so on.

Instead of proceeding in a columnar fashion the North Korean cryptographers used a variation on this method of additive generation by diagonally adding two lines of digits by alternating paths that reversed its path when the last column was reached. As follows, using non-carrying addition:

Column --> __1__2___3__4___5__6__7___8__9___0

Line One: 789 234 911 874 639 481 648 129 384 313
Line Two: 439 741 122 789 473 938 391 679 917 836
Line Three: 663 996 420 854 690 410 567 220 217 110
Line Four: 018 092 227 161 701 379 137 495 946 886

and so on until line fifty.

See the appendix for a more detailed description of this additive generation technique as well as a methodology to break it. The NKPA referred to this system in their messages as "The Crooked Line". In Tokyo I called it the "alternating diagonal generation" method, while the Arlington Hall cryptanalytic dilettanti in a Top Secret message triumphantly tagged it "Boustrophedonic Fibonacci". This confused the hell out of Captain Ligon, who was unaware of this methodology let alone a sixteenth century mathematician. He was never interested in memoranda I prepared of purely summary technological nature. To the best of my knowledge, these reports were never sent to Washington or anywhere else.

The March 1951 combined CCF and NKPA offensive had fizzled and they pulled back to more defensible positions. The Eighth Army followed cautiously. Seoul was recaptured and a period of insignificant military activity followed. This was also reflected in the cryptanalytic struggle. Nothing new except the North Korean command network predictably scheduled changes in their additive pad and a repagination of their codebook - both being easily parried, as they did not occur at the same time. That event would have been disastrous for communications intelligence.

At one point Eighth Army intelligence (G-2) lost track of the whereabouts of the 40th Chinese Army headquarters. A CCF Army designation was equivalent to a U. S. Army Corps. G-2 requested ASA to be alert to any mention of this formidable unit. At the 60th Sig in Korea a low-level battalion North Korean Army message was intercepted that was encoded in a simple system. It mentioned a farmer complaining that Chinese soldiers from the 40th Army were bivouacked in his orchard and eating all his produce. Captain Sam Hong, a hard working translator, picked up the message and bypassing the "Special Security Officers" (a.k.a. glorified messenger boys) drove a jeep himself to Eighth Army G-2 to report this news. It was gratefully received. This informal, swift relationship worked well, but was replaced later by a slower, more structured, bureaucratic, arrangement when ASA expanded in Korea.

Word was passed about that many of us were being recommended for medals. There were fifteen being mentioned for Bronze Stars and one - myself for a "Legion of Merit". This struck me as odd, as the Legion of Merit Medal was euphemistically called the "Officers

Good Conduct Medal" and usually awarded to a field grade officer when he finished a tour of duty - usually three years. Although I was now filling the organizational vacancy of a Colonel - "Theater Cryptanalyst", it was well known that a twenty year old Private First Class does not qualify.

In times of slow activity it was either go back to some stray unbroken systems or study Korean or Japanese using the big dictionaries and study material that was now available to us. One strange batch of messages involved transcriptions of "flashlight" traffic intercepted around Pusan harbor. It was thought to be espionage communications, but in all likelihood it was "Black Market" activity. We could never make head or tail of it.

Having little to do I dug out of my file cabinet the pre-war North Korean traffic. The messages just prior to the start of the war intrigued me. I started to translate, as best as I could; a message dated June 22, 1950. It was not the usual standardized army jargon, but a long-winded exhortation titled "combat order number 001" signed by Kim Il Sung himself. It involved the Fourth North Korean Division and mentioned the city of "Oui Jong Bu" which was south of the thirty-eighth parallel. I called Copeland over, showed it to him and asked him to check my translation so far. He grinned and said, "This is 'Pearl Harbor' type congressional investigation material".

Sgt. Dugan overheard us and walked over to my desk. I pointed out what I was doing and Cope repeated his statement and added "I'd like to get a copy to my Senator - Margaret Chase Smith, of Maine." Although Cope was speaking facetiously, never passing up a chance to plug his Native State, Dugan took it very seriously. Cope and I knew he would report this to Captain Ligon.

Dugan departed and we discussed the inability of the U. S. Army to come up with a single qualified cryptanalytic officer that would be a replacement for the incompetent Captain Ligon during the first year of the Korean War, the most critical time. [He was replaced in January 1952, then promoted to major when he returned to Arlington Hall and subsequently separated from the Military. He applied for employment with the National Security Agency, but he was rejected.]

The admission requirements of the Army Security Agency School probably had something to do with it. All enlisted students had to have an AGCT (Army General Classification Test) of over 110, as well as pass a cryptographic aptitude test. The AGCT score was roughly equivalent to an intelligence quotient (IQ) level. Officers merely had to be High School graduates to attend their brief "survey" course in cryptography. The enlisted men's rigorous course in Military Cryptanalysis of 17 weeks was comprehensive, demanding and well worth it. The textbooks were written by the grand daddy of American cryptologists Colonel William F. Friedman, with additional material composed at Arlington Hall by Lambros Demetrios Callimihos. Both men probably slept with a giant thesaurus for a pillow to absorb more verbose and obscure ways of expressing something. See the appendix for information from the ASA School catalog.

The structure of the United States Army revolves around the fundamental administrative unit known as the company - a grouping of about 200 men, with a company commander, company clerk, company supply sergeant and the man who ran the whole thing - the first sergeant. The organizational template for the company is the infantry rifle company, little changed since the Civil War in which the company is further subdivided into four rifle platoons each headed by a young lieutenant. Over a hundred years ago these officers were the best swordsmen, horsemen and probably the best marksmen in the company. Leadership was founded on military prowess, not by Act of Congress or political influence.

The only structured counterpart in the Army Security Agency was the Signal Service Company. An example was the 60th SSC, the first communications intelligence unit in Korea. In 1949 when based in Fort Lewis, Washington, it had strength of 170 men and a half dozen officers. The enlisted men were qualified in over thirty different military occupation specialties, with the predominant group being that of 68 morse code radio intercept operators - some were high speed radio operators undergoing on-the-job training. This would provide enough men to staff 17 intercept "positions" full time. That is three shifts of eight hours each with a fourth shift rotational for time off.

About 40 men were involved in basic logistical support - such as company administration, supply clerks, cooks, and security guards and since the unit was mobile, truck drivers. Although, in times of movement anybody could be designated as a truck driver as well as "volunteer" to strike and raise tents - like a traveling circus. The remaining men were involved in intelligence gathering support - radio equipment maintenance, radio direction finding, traffic analysis, shift supervision and a large communications center involving over 25 teletype and cryptographic machine operators. Notwithstanding the table of organization authorization for 3 cryptanalytic technicians – code breakers - none were present. When the 60th arrived in Korea in October 1950 it had been beefed-up with an additional 200 people. There were more intercept operators, about a dozen cryptanalytic techies led by Dick Copeland from ASAPAC in Tokyo and Jim McCloy from Vint Hill Farms in Virginia and about 10 Korean translators including officers, enlisted men and civilians. Later Chinese translators arrived and small radio direction finding detachments were split-off to remote locations.

In the 60th SSC the cryptanalysis technicians did not attempt to break into unreadable messages, but decoded traffic using solutions forwarded from Tokyo. Copeland and McCloy concentrated on plain text "chatter" between NKPA radio operators. They became so adept at this they became virtual translators, turning the standardized Morse code into Korean then into English. This took some of the load off of the translators and supplied the traffic analysts with worthwhile information. They worked closely with two translator/sergeants Danny Y. C. Lee and Campen, who were also becoming proficient in Mandarin Chinese.

The lower echelon radio communications between Chinese Communist army units were now being picked-up. A radio direction finding network was established to zero in on these transmissions. A wide base line was established with D/F detachments spread from one coast of Korea to the other, all directed by the 60th Signal Service Company. Some circuits were non-morse, voice only, just sending numbers - encrypted messages by verbalization. This required the presence of Chinese linguistic personnel, Americans from various "Chinatowns", who usually spoke Cantonese but were indoctrinated in the Mandarin dialect.

On one occasion members of the Third Infantry Division's 65th Regimental Combat Team from Puerto Rico "captured" a few "Chinese" along with one young Irish-American from Brooklyn. Luckily, Bill Reilly spoke some Spanish and explained to his baffled captors that they were all Americans from a radio intelligence intercept detachment and they were permitted to proceed.

The other Signal Service Companies based in Japan, the 126th in Kyoto and the 111th on Okinawa were structured similarly to the 60th. A "small" Signal Service Detachment, the 51st, in Chitose on the Northern Japanese Island of Hokkaido, had grown in size to over

200 men. It was located in an ideal area for intercepting Korean, Chinese and Russian radio transmissions and became extremely productive.

Headquarters and Headquarters Company, Army Security Agency - Pacific, in northern Tokyo had grown to over 500 men, including Japanese personnel staffing non-classified positions as cooks, truck drivers, security guards as well as waitresses and bartenders. Officers with nothing better to do treated the company as if it was infantry. There was a re-hash of basic training subjects including close order drill, calisthenics, map reading, rifle firing qualification, small infantry unit tactics and so on. Obviously, no soldier should let himself or his basic skills fall into disuse, but this nonsense soon got out of hand, as a new company executive officer, Jack Gentry intended "to whip this outfit into shape".

First Lieutenant Gentry requested from Colonel Greiner authorization every Saturday for a full dress military inspection and review. The Colonel ordered every thing shut down including the communications center and all intercept operations. One radio intercept operator appended a comment to the North Korean message he was interrupted from completely copying - "I have to stop now to change uniforms and put on white gloves for a parade. I wonder what the guys in the foxholes in Korea think about this". The intercept was transmitted verbatim to Washington which caused a reprimand to be sent to Colonel Greiner. Just shutting down a "command level" communications center alone should have resulted in a courts-martial. The Colonel was oblivious to the mission of the Army Security Agency.

In the combat branches of the military, such as infantry, there is a dramatic "Darwinian" influence on the conduct of officers. If an incompetent or cowardly officer is not observed and removed by his superiors the enemy usually disposes of him. Unfortunately, some good men are also killed or wounded along with the "bad apple" officer. If this "normal" process of elimination fails to occur, the derelict officer receives a bullet in the back from one of his own men. This unfortunate and brutal fact reached alarming proportions during the Viet Namm war where it was referred to as "Fragging". We often speculated on how long the illiterate Lieutenant Jack Gentry would last in a real rifle company, and who would get him first the enemy or his own men. Instead, he was promoted to Captain.

Officers relieved of combat commands gravitated to rear echelon assignments such as the Army Security Agency. The most ignominious posting for an officer was to command and all Black military unit as the United States Army was not desegregated until 1948 by Executive order from President Harry Truman. [Army Security Agency units were not desegregated until the late nineteen fifties].

On April 11th we were all startled by the news that President Truman had cashiered General MacArthur. All GHQ troops were ordered to form a guard of honor for his departure - lining the streets of Tokyo along his route to Haneda Airport. ASA personnel as usual were exempt from this duty, which would have been entertaining. One enterprising GI, received his PX ration of American cigarettes in the brand of "Parliament". He resold the individual packs at a big profit to the Japanese who preferred "Chesterfields" by the carton, saying that "Parliaments" were MacArthur's personal brand.

Out of the blue, Captain Ligon came over to me and stated that we were both going on a trip to our intercept station at Chitose on the northernmost island of Japan - Hokkaido. It was ostensibly a morale building trip to familiarize the intercept operators and traffic analysts with our successes in reading North Korean communications. The men were working long hours on rotating shifts copying the traffic of enemy operators who were transmitting long, dull, groups of four-digit messages. Any Korean "chatter" between radio operators was unintelligible, so the intercept-operators were naturally concerned over the value of their arduous work. There was a rumor circulated among intercept operators that only the first and last ten groups of a message were important as everything was transmitted in unbreakable codes- nothing was further from the truth.

I asked if only Chitose was involved. He replied that shortly Sergeants Hawkins and Dugan would accompany him to the 126th in Kyoto and then fly down to the 111th on Okinawa. Since there were other Sergeants available in the section and there was a smoldering mutual animosity between myself and the Captain, it struck me as rather odd that he picked me. After the trip I was to find out the real reason.

The captain had prepared some large charts depicting blown-up sample messages with the four-digit groups decoded into Korean and the rough translation. All stamped top-secret - "CODEWORD" -the actual code word "COPSE" was not written as it was classified itself. We rolled the charts into a cylinder that I had to carry. I strapped on a 45-caliber army issue automatic as we were now an Officer-enlisted man courier team transporting Top Secret material.

We left Tokyo on the "Yankee limited" a military train commandeered from the Japanese Railway system that ran daily to Northern Honshu and via railway-ferry to Hakodate on the Island of Hokkaido. The "Dixie Limited" was the counterpart that headed south to Osaka and Kyoto. It was a pleasant overnight trip with first-class accommodations. I had to sleep with the cylinder in the top bunk of our compartment. The food was excellent in the dining car, as we conducted a strained conversation revolving around Japanese culture, language and the pretty countryside. We made a presentation with the charts immediately on arriving at the ASA Chitose intercept unit - garrisoned at an American Air Force Base.

After chow that evening I stopped into the small Enlisted Men's club to catch up with some old friends I knew from other ASA posts and the signal schools back in the states. It was a plush layout with pretty waitresses that spent more time sitting and chatting with the GI's then delivering beer. I relaxed with a bottle of beer on a couch with my feet up on a small table having a conversation with a waitress possessing the remote northern Japanese dialect. All of a sudden an Air Force MP walks up and raps his club on the sole of my boot shouting "You may lounge around like that in Tokyo, you don't do it here". I jumped up startled, then heard the MP laugh and he was joined by a bunch at the bar when I noticed Sergeant Woods an old buddy from Tokyo emerge from the group and saunter over twirling his MP club. He was a member of a two man joint Army-Air force MP patrol that policed the local base and environs. It was obvious that Woods had set his coworker up to bug me. After everybody had a good laugh, Woods told me to meet him at another place when he got off patrol.

I was sitting at the bar when a sergeant I had noticed at today's pep talk came up to me and offered to buy me a Sapporo beer. He asked "If that whole presentation was a crock of BS". I told him it was pretty much a cooked-up charade, with nothing specific or real on display even though it was marked TOP SECRET – Code Word. He replied that was what he thought. Usually, when two ASA people that are unfamiliar to each other meet off duty, there is a series of sparring questions as a preliminary. This is to smoke out a spook that is looking for a blabbermouth to report for violating security. The existence of these investigators from SID (Security Investigation Division) is overly exaggerated and even when rarely encountered they usually tip their hand by demonstrating their complete lack of knowledge about the particulars of the communications intelligence mission - just dropping a few general terms. The aura of undercover agents being present contributes to the sham-security that permeates everything in the "Intelligence Community".

We hit it off quickly. He had been a trick-chief intercept operator who was undergoing on-the-job training as a Traffic Analyst. He asked if we really had broken all the systems of the North Koreans. I told him all but one, the political security net that came up on the first of the year that I was still working on. This was the first chance I had to talk with someone knowledgeable about the actual first step of the job, message collecting. For him it was the initial exposure to a working cryptanalyst, a job he hoped to be trained for someday.

He had been on the assignment in Chitose for over a year and was on duty the night the North Koreans jumped across the 38th parallel. I asked if he or someone he knew coined the code word "GIZMO" to identify the traffic. He had heard of it, it was no one that he knew. I said probably someone in the 126th -Kyoto, who should get a medal.

During further beer consumption, we discussed the Russian and Chinese problems and inevitably, the pre-war North Korean networks. He had intercepted some of the FE00x (unidentified) messages as he had frequently been a search operator – scanning the radio spectrum for new traffic. He was not surprised when I told him I had broken it and that it was indeed North Korean military material. He related that their direction finding had placed it in the same area as the Russian 9th Air Army, which was either North Korea or Manchuria - almost due West from their D/F site. He also noted that the procedure signals and chatter of "GIZMO" was the same as the pre-war stuff. I was impressed by the assumptions that he and the other interceptors made on what some of the Korean plain text meant. This was "Chatter" – the procedural exchanges between North Korean operators sometimes asking to repeat a group, switch frequencies, and like matters.

We agreed on the "Pearl Harbor" aspect of these messages and the implications for the Agency if there was ever an investigation. That would have to wait, as there were more pressing things at this time. I mentioned that back in Tokyo I had a folder of about eighty messages that I still work on. He recalled that they had intercepted many more and that I should stop in the radio hut tomorrow and he would show me the logs.

We dropped the subject, when two other guys I knew came over to tell me that Woody was waiting for me. I asked them what kind of a place was it where he hangs up his armband, 45 and billy club. They said that I was in for trouble and would be lucky to be able to get out alive. I asked my newfound buddy to come along, but he said he had an early day and would see me tomorrow.

The next day, after the morning cheer leading session before a group of about twenty very-sleepy "ditty-boppers" who had just gotten off their night-trick, I stopped by to locate my beer-buddy from the night before. He had the intercept logs for the first six months of 1950 stacked up on his desk. He said thanks for the clue-in last night and that he had passed the word to the other guys. I started going over the logs and there were about two hundred intercepts that were positive or probable pre-war NKPA. He had lightly ticked off in pencil those that he knew of. I asked him was there any way we could identify duplicates or re-transmissions, he said no-can-do. The entries for June 1950 interested me so I wrote down the dates and the group counts on the back of an envelope. I would compare their records with what I had in my file in Tokyo. I folded the paper and placed it my breast pocket.

Two other 709's (Traffic Analysts) and the trick chief came over and we talked in general about North Korean matters. I complimented them on their plain text procedural assumptions and spelled out in Korean what some of them literally meant. There were Russian translators available, but no Korean. No helpful explanations came from Washington or Tokyo - the men operated in the dark and did very well.

Just then Captain Ligon came into the room and noticed the logbooks. He asked what I was doing and I stated that we were discussing NKPA procedural terminology and started to give examples. The Korean language was beyond him. He waved me off and said with an unctuous smile "I'm sure these men have a lot of work to do. You're lucky. You can take the rest of the day off -no session this afternoon. Why don't you go into Chitose and do some sight-seeing." I replied "OK by me. I'll see what the town looks like in the light of day. See you guys later". They laughed as I left the office. I patted my pocket with the folded envelope and said to myself "mission accomplished".

Arriving back in the office in Tokyo the first item on the agenda was to compare the log extract with the traffic in my file cabinet. Capt. Ligon was not in the office, I opened the drawer in my "unlocked" file cabinet and found that the folder with the pre-war traffic was missing. I turned and inquired if anyone had removed a file from my cabinet. Lt. Toft got up from her desk, blushed and scampered out of the office. Nobody answered, some just shook their heads. I asked Cope if there had been a routine classified trash "burn" last week. He nodded and said "yea". I slammed the draw shut and swore. The pre-war North Korean messages had gone up in flames. It was now clear why I was asked to go to

Chitose. There would be no evidence available for a "Pearl Harbor" investigation.

I didn't have much of an opportunity to inquire further into the status of the pre-war traffic as I was ordered to Korea.

Chapter VII

- Flight to Taegu, Korea
  - Recovery of full page of additive
    - Eighth Army moves back to Seoul---

The author at K-37 Airstrip, Taegu, Korea May 1951.

On May 1st I was informed that I was to fly to Korea on temporary duty with the 60th Signal Service Company. Accordingly, my immunization record was brought up to date with two inoculations in one arm and three in the other, went to the supply room to draw a weapon as required and was handed an M-1 "Garand" rifle with bayonet. I thought it was a joke, but was assured that it was now necessary as they had run out of the smaller, lighter carbines.

In May-1951 the 60th Signal Service Company was located at a small airstrip, K-37, just outside of Taegu, Korea. The sixtieth sig had a tent city compound within a barbed wire security fence. The long running TV show "MASH" was genuinely accurate in the depiction of a typical army unit in the field. It was very much like that at the sixtieth, with the sad absence of anything approaching the likes of Major "Hot Lips Houlihan".

On May 5th I flew from Tokyo's Haneda airport aboard a C-54 with blood stained stretchers as seats along the walls of the aircraft. The aircraft was on a return trip from Tokyo Army Hospital. We landed at the huge K-2 air base at Taegu as fighter jets were taking off from the parallel runway. I reported to the gregarious Captain Don Mulvey the commanding officer of the 60th. He welcomed me saying "we always need more Korean translators". I realized that he was a lightweight as far as COMINT was concerned, but I didn't have the heart to set him straight because he was so pleasant. I left the CO's office-tent with a tent assignment and ran into old buddy from Tokyo Gene Scarborough who was convulsed with laughter when he spotted me with an M-1 rifle slung over my shoulder. "What the hell are you doing with that heavy artillery?" he asked, "Or have you been kicked out of the Agency into the infantry." I replied "Consider the war as good as over now that I'm here" as he escorted me to a large ten-man tent, where I stowed my duffel bag on a small collapsible cot. Gene later arranged for me to obtain a much lighter carbine.

I then reported to Captain Youn P. Kim in operations to get down to business. Things were run informally and much more differently in Korea than the spit-and-polish, “compartmented” bureaucracy of Headquarters in Tokyo, with a noticeable leap in morale. Everybody pitched in to help one another and went by first names including the officers. Captain Kim introduced me around the large tent and said "Work any hours you want, you know what you have to do. Most of the stuff comes in at night". Kim was frequently absent between translation duties, either at Eighth army intelligence (G-2) or at the 501st communications battalion bivouacked nearby. This was the embryo of the future large ASA units that were soon to be mobilized in Korea. He instructed another young translator, Lieutenant Lee, that in his absence to sign and authorize any message I composed to be sent to Washington and Tokyo, even if he didn't understand it. Dick Chun greeted me as he was making notations on a lead acetate overlay of a map of the front lines pasted on the wall of the tent. "John, It is still a yo-yo war. Look at this", as he indicated the up and down movements of the various contending military units. He then added "Come over to my tent later for a drink and sing-along". Dick had brought his guitar with him to Korea.

The Chinese Peoples Volunteer Army had just exhausted the spring offensive that started on April 22nd. Extremely heavy casualties and major supply problems caused them to go on the defensive and withdraw from the line in some areas. It was now the turn of the reconstituted North Korean Peoples Army to launch an offensive.

Two thirds of the line opposing the United Nations forces was now manned by the NKPA, with the First

Marine Division adjacent to the 187th Airborne Regimental Combat Team in the line directly opposing the enemy spearhead. I first became aware of this while decrypting a NKPA message that described the units in opposition as the American Marines and the number 187th parachute regiment. Information that was obtained from a few captured U. S. prisoners.

I interrupted the pervasive silence in the operations tent by jumping up from my table and shouting "This is serious! The jarhead-marines are next to the hopscotch-airborne. They'll be killing each other". Jokingly, we all thought the Marines and the Airborne would fight each other as they usually do in barroom brawls, today they didn't. Instead, they concentrated on the North Koreans and blunted the attack.

Army Security Agency units were completely deciphering and translating the messages of the Command Network of the NKPA. However, the "In Min Gun" was scheduling a cryptosystem change, called the "Crooked Line" cipher, to coincide with their offensive. A blackout of valuable intelligence at this time would prove menacing.

One morning, at around six A.M., Corporal Milton Pagel, a cryptanalytic technician, entered the pyramidal tent and shook me awake. "John,-- John. They have started the new system. There are two messages coming in now, we can't read them." I replied "OK, I'll be right over", As I donned my fatigue uniform, laced up my combat boots, and walked over to the large intercept tent.

Several intercept operators were banging away at their "mill" typewriters, recording the four digit groups of radio signals. In front of two operators the unfurled roll of multipart canary yellow paper was dropping to the wooden slats on the floor of the tent.

Pagel pointed and whispered "This one is over 600 groups and that one is over a thousand." I replied "OK,

Uncle Milty, you take the little one. If it is what I think it is, we'll recover a full additive page in one shot. All we need is the first two lines."

We each moved a chair close to an operator, picked up the roll of paper and endeavored to decrypt the beginning of the two messages. From the call signs of the traffic it was known who was the internal addressee, as well as the signatories. The messages were from two North Korean Corps Headquarters reporting their situation to NKPA advanced headquarters. After the first twenty groups of both messages were decoded the entire 500-group pad could be formulated from the "crooked line" technique of generation. The results were confirmed by the text of the two messages, both having had to "doubled-back" and re-use the additive as they were in excess of 500 groups.

Although, the North Koreans transmitted in four digit groups, they were only using a three-digit code. The fourth digit was a sum check -either for validating the radio transmission or the encryption process. We never figured out that part. It was unnecessary. We split the second copy from the two communications, decoded them completely and had them ready for translation before the North Korean receiving operators acknowledged receipt for the transmissions. They usually sent every message twice, as the intercept operators cut the roll of paper and placed the beginning of the messages back into the typewriters. On the second transmission they merely listened to the Morse characters and typed in a correction if it differed from the first transmission.

The copy was very clear this morning, free of garbles due to interference either man-made or atmospheric. If there were a difference between the two transmissions the operators would hunt us down and bring it to our attention. This was all unwritten and unofficial procedure everyone instinctively understood it.

There would be no intelligence blackout today. By eight-thirty a full 500 group three-digit additive pad was recovered, typed up and ready for transmission to Tokyo and Arlington Hall.

I pinned a note to the message to transmit exactly as typed precisely 10 groups to the line to demonstrate clearly the generation method. I had Lt. Lee sign the message, carried it to the comm-center then went to the mess-tent for breakfast. I found Gene Scarborough and Johnny Cardinal and sat down next to them. They were planning to go swimming at a nearby reservoir that day. Cardinal asked me to join them if I was off for the day. I replied "finished for the day".

After a while one of the comm-center guys wandered in and sat down. He was wearing only a T-shirt and mumbling about all the work he had just done. He was slurring his words in a Texas drawl, saying, "Nobody tells me how to send a message. Some joe-jemoke says transmit ten groups to the line". He was a well-known drunk, Sgt. "Gabe" Gabriel, and obviously still soused. I told him "those were my instructions". He said "well I didn't send it like you said". I got up from the table saying "you stupid son-of-a-bitch, that was probably the most important message you ever sent". He replied" Hey, you can't talk to me like that. I'm a sergeant". I snapped "you might not be much longer", grabbed my breakfast tray and headed out of the tent to find Captain Kim. Gabe tried to focus his eyes and asked Cardinal "Who the hell does he think he is?". Johnny replied in mocking pidgin-Korean "Him Number one code-break boy". Gabriel looked at Scarborough and asked, "Can he really have me busted?". Gene replied, "You're in deep shit, Tex".

I went back to the operations tent and found the confirmation copy of the message. The groups were spread out all over the page. Captain Kim was still translating the larger North Korean message as I explained what happened - "Those comm-center guys have got to stop drinking on the job." Captain Kim laughed and said he would speak to Captain Mulvey, the Company commander. Kim asked if we should retransmit the message. I replied "No, Cope will figure it out in Tokyo, that's important in case they pick-up a message that we haven't. That happens a lot. Arlington Hall is on their own".

The next day Capt. Mulvey called in the NCOIC (non-commissioned officer-in-charge) of the communications center and told them to lay off the booze. The sergeant replied "OK, we only have a few bottles left. After that we'll stop".

On May 18th the last mammoth Chinese attack centered on the 2nd Division, just north of Wonju. The daily G-3 (Operations) report stated that artillery, predominately under X Corps command claimed, over 10,000 Chinese infantry killed in one day. Mobile 155 Millimeter "Long Tom" guns arrayed hub-cap-to-hub-cap, and joined by coordinated FEAF air strikes decimated the closely grouped Chinese regiments. North Korean divisions were frantically ordered in to cover the withdrawal of the Chinese Armies.

During the new lull in the fighting we would just sit around the operations tent and shoot the breeze. The subject of the pre-war North Korean traffic came up. I was still strongly critical about the failure of ASAPAC to translate and submit those messages to higher headquarters. Valuable intelligence about the North Korean Army and their bases that the "Chinese Volunteers" was now using was withheld. A civilian Korean translator Erskine St. Clair said, "What do you want to do start another Pearl Harbor investigation?" I replied, "I don't think that's possible, the traffic was destroyed."

The 60th Sig was ordered to move north with Eighth Army Headquarters as it advanced to Seoul. The last Chinese and North Korean offensive ground to a halt and Eighth Army went over to the offensive. After massive artillery barrages, the American and South Korean Divisions moved into positions vacated by the devastated enemy. The North Koreans screened the withdrawal of the Chinese and every night their major command network reported the situation. The NKPA headquarters would then issue orders for the next days movement, until the front stabilized along lines that would pretty much remain the same for the rest of the War.

On June 1st EUSAK (main) re-occupied Seoul and the 60th SSC followed suit. It was a bright, sunny morning as we struck our pyramidal, ten man tents and loaded up the trucks. My friend from the motor pool Kenny Cole designated me as his assistant driver to sit up front with him. I had obtained a pair of goggles to put on top of my steel helmet like General Rommel as well as a bright yellow scarf that the troopers of the First Cavalry Division wore during parades. That didn't impress some of the grumbling sergeants riding in the rear of the truck as they knew damn well I didn't know how to drive a truck.

Captain Don Mulvey, with a can of Budweiser beer in his hand, waved the convoy of sixteen World War II vintage trucks out of the compound at 6 am. Only five made it to Seoul as a group as the long 210-mile trip took its toll on the World War II vintage trucks. Each truck was pulling a trailer loaded down with equipment, tents and tent poles. Between Taegu and Waegwan the trucks were grinding their gears as we passed over a mountain range. The dusty roadside in and around Taejon was littered with blown up and burnt out Russian T-34 tanks, including two that were painted with words indicating they were personally knocked out by General Dean before his capture in July of 1950. Further along, there was a great deal of damaged and abandoned American trucks, jeeps and one tank.

At Taejon we stopped for a lunch of C-rations and noticed a flat tire. We used our only spare and without a jack we used rocks and tent poles to prop up the rear of the truck. The convoy moved out and we were on our own. It was a picnic like holiday as we now moved through the Korean countryside, except for the men in the rear of the truck who were covered with dust. Just outside of Pyongtaek we had a blowout in our right front tire. Without a spare, we had to take a tire from the one of the four dual tires in the rear and use rocks and tent poles again.

At Suwon we passed a large convoy of spanking new trucks and jeeps that had pulled over and were lined up hubcap-to-hubcap. It was the main body of General Van Fleet's Eight Army Headquarters as many of the jeeps sported large generals stars and everybody was in spit and polish, carefully pressed fatigue uniforms. They were having what looked like a catered lunch - it definitely was not C-rations. Our dirty, broken down truck received quizzical looks as we bounced by and I leaned out sporting my goggles and flowing yellow scarf shouting "Onward, men" pointing North "to the front".

We were again delayed outside of YungDungPo by a Military Policeman directing traffic. He pulled us over saying that we were speeding and heading in the wrong direction for EUSAK headquarters in Seoul. Kenny told him we were late for our dinner dates and we knew the exact location of our destination. The MP became officious and walked around to look into the truck and trailer. I got out and followed him as he poked into the trailer and peered into the truck. I informed him that he was not authorized to see what was in there as he would be violating the Espionage Act and Army Regulation 380-5. I started to rattle off the litany of regulation that was ingrained in all ASA personnel "No person is authorized solely by grade or position access to classified information....". He said "Hold it, wise guy, where is the orders or trip ticket for this truck". We didn't have anything, as the sergeant holding the orders switched trucks after our second flat tire. I had a copy of my detached service orders in my pocket, indicating I was on an Army Security Agency mission. He frowned as he looked over the one-page order. I said, "You will notice that it's signed by General Ridgway". His attitude changed as he handed back the paper and said, "I see, you guys should know better not to speed like that. There were a lot of gooks killed on the road along here". I said thanks, climbed into the truck and as we pulled away the guys in the back of the truck gave him the finger.

It was nearing dusk as we approached our specified destination in the western suburbs of Seoul. It was a former ASA radio intercept site that had been established during the occupation of South Korea in 1946 consisting of a few concrete buildings, that had been vacated several times, but still had a usable antenna field.

There were only a few trucks there, including a portable intercept truck that was full of sweating, ear-phoned, radio intercept operators banging away at their typewriters. The trick chief informed us that the rest of the convoy had gone to a High School in Seoul, without leaving directions. Furthermore there was guerrilla activity, the surrounding area was heavily mined and was considered too dangerous. He said a courier jeep would be out in the morning to pick up the night's message "take" and lead us to the new site.

There was one other truck from our original convoy. The rest was an advanced party that came up two days earlier to maintain continuous monitoring of the enemy circuits and were supposed to move out in the morning to join-up with the main group. There were no officers around. The trick chief was a technical sergeant, the highest ranking enlisted man present, and suggested we not try to make it into Seoul after dark - there were no street lights and there still is a lot of gun-fire at night.

We talked it over with the guys from the other truck, including the driver Jack Karlin. Jack, an old New York buddy, thought he could find the High School if we got telephone instructions. The tech. sergeant said the nearest field phone was at the combat Military Police point back at where the road split off from the main highway. We laughed and all agreed to stay the night. Jack Karlin said "Oh, he stopped you for speeding too."

The trick chief looked relieved and thought it would be a good idea if we set two men on guard duty around the perimeter during the night. He said the radiomen were working 12 hour shifts and would feel much better if there was a sentry or two around. There were sixteen of us that were available for guard duty from the two convoy trucks so we ran a quick pool to take an hour each. I drew out of helmet the 3am to 4 slot.

We also had a 30-caliber machine gun that was set up in a mount on one of the trucks. We dug out our cots and one-man sleeping bags, had a cold dinner of C-rations, and bunked in one of the buildings. There was some gunfire and shouting off in the distance around 10 o'clock, nothing came of it. Before I dozed off again I cradled my rifle between my legs.

It was a little chilly and very quiet during my hour on guard. After my relief showed up I stopped off in the intercept hut-on-the-truck were it was much warmer. There was only one operator copying. I looked over his shoulder and noticed it was a short message on the NKPA supply net. Two other operators had their headsets on, were head-down, eyes-closed, resting on their typewriters.

The rest were smoking and drinking coffee. The trick chief was still up and told me "very little traffic tonight." I asked about the critical North Korean Corps circuit. He reached into the wire basket and pulled out one short forty-five-group message. The call signs indicated it was the Third Corps Commander sending to NKPA Headquarters. I said "This is awfully short for this guy. He is usually over 500 groups in his daily report." He appeared a little bewildered and asked, "Is this stuff any good? Is it really worth all the effort we put in?" I replied "This net in particular is worth its weight in gold."

He looked a little happier and offered me a cup of coffee. I borrowed a pencil from him and on a slip of paper decoded the first few groups of the message. I just wanted to make sure the additive key or the underlying code had not changed. It hadn't, so there was no need for me to go work that early in the morning. He shook his head in incredulity, as I told him it was a routine report that would be fully decoded, translated and dispatched to G-2 at EUSAK main later that morning.

The next day we arrived at a Korean High School in Northern Seoul, joined the others and set up shop. We slept and worked in classrooms with furniture that we looted from the surrounding well-to-do community.

North Korean intercepts dropped considerably as there was talk of an armistice. We had an opportunity to move around and sightsee Seoul. The war was grinding to a halt with only the faint thundering and flashes of nightly artillery bombardments and the midnight bombing forays of "Bed-Check-Charlie" to remind us that there was still a war.

Chapter VIII

July through October 1951

- Return to Tokyo, Award of the Bronze Star Medal-

- Cryptographic Oddity -

- The "Iron Curtain" comes down on COMINT -

- Movin' On -

<u>Headlines from Pacific Stars and Stripes, July 1951</u>

- Kaesong cease fire negotiations underway
- Seventeen Japanese and Koreans were found guilty of espionage by an allied international provost court
- Rita Hayworth accepts settlement in her divorce from Aly Kahn
- Church services now scheduled at the 1st Tokyo Arsenal (ASAPAC)
- Jack Benny entertains the troops with his show at the Ernie Pyle theater in Tokyo-Jersey Joe Walcott KO's Ezzard Charles for the heavyweight boxing title- - Korean War sputters like damp firecracker/ FEAF sorties lowest in a year
- Accordionist Dick Contino pleads guilty to draft dodging
- U. S. State department refuses to tell Senator Joseph McCarthy (R. Wis.) the status of loyalty cases involving its employees
- Last all Negro Regiment the 24th in Korea to be disbanded
- ATIS(Allied Translator Interpreter Service) upsets ASAPAC in GHQ softball tourney, 4-3 at Doolittle field
- Movie: "The Bullfighter and the Lady" Robert Stack and Gina Roland.

Word came from Tokyo that it was time for my return. I packed up my belongings and arranged for transportation to Kimpo air base and a flight back to Haneda, Japan. In the morning, I stopped by the operations classroom before leaving to say goodbye and see if anything new came in the night before. All was silent, so I briefly skimmed the G-3 operations report. I noticed on the map that defending the Western end of the line and also protecting Kimpo, was a tank platoon from the British Commonwealth Brigade. On the road to Kimpo my jeep passed three "Centurion" tanks going in the other direction. I guessed that Kimpo was now probably undefended.

The air operations at a dirty "Quonset hut" at Kimpo was jammed with all sorts of people trying to get back to Japan. An unusual early season typhoon was heading for Honshu and the only flights were to Ashiya (J-1) on the southernmost Japanese Island of Kyushu. The priority level on my orders permitted me to bump a U. S. Army Major and get on the next C-54 to Ashiya. He had on the weirdest uniform I've ever seen and was lugging a high-powered hunting rifle with a telescopic sight. He was probably going to Japan on R and R and planned to do some hunting. He gave me a nasty look as I brushed past him and I grinned back as I climbed up the steps to the plane.

We sat on bloodstained stretchers along the walls of the aircraft with our gear and weapons spread out on the floor. This plane was also used to evacuate wounded, which gave one an eerie feeling. I noticed some intercept operators from the 60th signal who had boarded earlier and went over to talk with them. They were heading to Tokyo for a week's R and R.

The crew was friendly and invited those that were interested to come up to the cockpit two at a time to have a look. Most everybody on board was sleeping, so one of the intercept operators and I went up. There were extra sets of earphones on a table and my companion asked if we could put them on. The radio operator said "Sure!" The clouds had lifted as we approached Ashiya. A brilliant late afternoon sunlight brightened the lush greenery of Japan and the endless line of parked military transports that stretched out before us. The radio operator tapped out a short message - "INT CHOW" or "What is on the menu for dinner?" The reply came back "ICE CREAM". I asked him was that was some sort of operational code, he just laughed and said, "No, it was all I had to do all day". I thought of the grim messages that the Korean and Russian aircraft exchanged. We were being initiated into the country club world of the U. S. Air Force.

On the ground we were told the only way to Tokyo was by a train that would be leaving after midnight. We had seven hours to kill, so we wandered around the sprawling base. We stopped by the enlisted men's service club where there was a party and dance going on complete with a Carmen Miranda type floor how. At the door a corporal said "We are sorry, but since you do not have class "A" uniforms (khaki) on, you are not permitted to enter". So much for the Air Force.

I asked my newfound companions if anybody had an empty duffel bag or something similar. One said yes, he had brought one to bring back souvenirs from Japan. I said get it and well go off base and fill up the bag with bottles of beer. Just outside the gate was the usual array of little bars and sake houses. We picked out one, went in and relaxed for a few hours.

My new found comrades had never been to Japan coming straight to Pusan, Korea by troopship, so I filled them in on the lay-of-the-land. We found out that we had many friends in common from radio operator and the other ASA schools in the states. We pooled our yen and purchased a supply of beer to last on our two-day train trip to Tokyo. It was a relaxing and enjoyable trip.

The front lines were beginning to look more like the World War One "trench warfare" predicament. Both the Chinese and North Korean armies reported to a "Combined Headquarters" in Pyongyang. The NKPA was still under the command of Kim Il Sung, with Nam Il as his chief of staff, both men sometimes originating messages that was in their enciphered three digit code. General Kim Ung, with Kim Kwang Hyop as the chief of Staff, directing the II, III, and V Corps commanded the “front-line” headquarters. Many messages were sent between these units and were intercepted by ASA units then swiftly decoded, translated and forwarded to Eighth Army headquarters and GHQ in Tokyo. The remaining five Corps were now in reserve. Peng Teh-huai commanded the CCF. His deputy commander was Teng Hua. Their headquarters was in Shenyang, Manchuria with a Teletype link via landlines to Pyongyang. We intercepted none of their communications.

On July 21st General Orders was received from GHQ awarding two Lt. Colonels, two Majors and myself the Bronze Star Medal. I was called in to see Lt. Colonel Sills the executive officer of ASAPAC. He was very somber and impressed upon me the honor I was about to receive. Although, he indicated that he did not quite understand what the intentionally vague citation was for. Then his eyes lit up and he said we would have a parade next Saturday. He went over the protocol for the parade and the review, and where everybody would stand, and the band would play, and photographs would be taken. His branch of service was the cavalry (now armor) and I had the distinct feeling he would rather have this grandiose military review on horseback.

The presentation and parade came off on schedule on July 28th, most of my friends resented the spit-and-polish dress uniforms and the time taken from their Saturday day off. Nonetheless, we celebrated in the Enlisted men's' club that afternoon.

On Monday it was back on the job, where things were uneventful until mid August. Then, one of the strangest encryption systems in the history of cryptology appeared. A NKPA supply echelon was transmitting traffic that appeared to be plain text, but made no coherent sense. The message preamble specified the group count, which was the count of Korean language syllables. A group count was only sent with encrypted messages. A translator brought a few messages to me saying "This is not translatable, It's not plain text". I looked at it, agreed with him and started to study them. It was a low priority network and since there was no other tactical problem traffic at the time I had the opportunity to examine the messages. Initially, I rejected it as a substitution system, as the North Korean's always used numeric methods. Alternatively, it could be transposed syllables. Anagramming up a message in columnar fashion, typical text appeared. It was a simple transposition rectangle, with a key phrase indicating the columnar transcription sequence. The key phrase was embedded in the text. The phrase was "Chung Guk In Min Gun Man Sei" or "long live the Korean people's army". I applied the key to the other messages and that quickly made sense out of the plain text. I took the traffic back to the translator and explained the system. Several messages were internally addressed to the "Comrade the Supreme Commander of the Department of Supply". He was unsure if he should include the key phrase "Long Live the Korean People's Army" in his translation. I suggested he make it a footnote. It appeared as the key for the rest of the month.

As I typed up the solution for transmission to Washington I embellished the description of this "Mickey

Mouse" system with the most polysyllabic, arcane and technologically obscure terminology I could devise: "monophase syllabic transposition"; "ultra-patriotic congruous specific communication determinant"; "structural indicator unmanifested". This was in the tradition of William F. Friedman (affectionately dubbed Uncle Willie), Lambros Demetrios Callimahos and the other dilettante cryptanalysts that inhabited Arlington Hall. The reply was a terse "thank you" for a true cryptologic oddity.

Many men from the 60th Signal Service Company were rotating back to the States or to Tokyo. Those with the most "points" or time in Korea were passing through ASAPAC on their way back home. Captain Mulvey, the former commanding officer of the 60th, took over Headquarters Company ASAPAC, in Tokyo. Captain Ben McKibben left ASAPAC and assumed command of the 60th SSC. A large Japanese hotel and gardens just outside the post was booked for several days to throw a "Sayonara" party. It was quite a party, lasting three days.

The cryptanalysis technicians from the 60th were not well received in operations by Captain Ligon. He resented their informality and in depth experience acquired in the combat zone of Korea. He assigned them to tasks well below their qualifications. World War Two veteran Sergeant Joe Chaney applied for and received a commission as a second lieutenant. He was soon back in Korea. Jim McCloy put in for a transfer to become sergeant of the security guard. Captain Ligon accepted and approved the transfer without even looking at it, and Jim was gone a day later. Morale in the codebreaking section was at an all time low.

I took a six-day furlough the first week of September and returned to a communications intelligence disaster. The North Korean Army command network improved their transmission security. They switched frequencies more often, cut out plain text chatter and transmitted in five digit groups. Our South Korean compatriots - sometimes known as “Kim’s Group” or “ROKM” (Republic of Korea Unit “M”) picked up the first messages of this new practice. They had detected the switch in frequency before the ASA units in Korea or Japan.

Flimsy carbon copies of their hand written intercepts were forwarded daily by courier to Tokyo from their unit in Seoul. I was filled with a sense of foreboding as I examined a few of the five digit messages. Five digit groups usually mean true "One Time Pad" - that is a theoretic unbreakable system. Sure enough the traffic manifested no exploitable patterns. It was completely random - the "Iron Curtain" was coming down on the cryptologic part of the War.

As the armistice negotiations dragged on and the contending land armies ground each other to a halt, the Air War picked up. "Relentless pressure" on the enemy must be maintained. Air power would do what the UN command (really the Pentagon) was unable to accomplish on the ground due to the unacceptability of further casualties. Both the U. S. Air Force and Navy strategic air power advocates argued that their means would bring the enemy to its knees. Accordingly, for domestic American political and inter-service public relations reasons a compromise was worked out. North Korea was split down the middle with the U.S. Air Force and other ground-based allied air units allocated the Western portion, while the U.S Navy in conjunction with surface vessels, targeted the Eastern sector.

This was easier said than done. The Russian MIG-15 was superior to the American F-86. According to Air Force public relations officers only the peerless training and tactics of U. S. pilots made the difference. Nevertheless, the PRO flak's semantic equivocation "Air

Superiority" was in jeopardy. The World War II vintage B-29's were no match for the MIG-15 and were forced to abandon day-light sorties around the Yalu river and the Northern reaches of Western Korea. Fighter protection by F-86's was limited by flying a long distance from their bases, thus having little fuel left for activities in the target areas.

Interception of Chinese messages in a variation of the venerable "Ming" code (CTC - Chinese telegraphic code) reported massive flights of MIG's from Shenyang (formerly Mukden) and other bases in Manchuria. Sometimes up to sixty aircraft were ordered to "do battle" over Korea against perhaps a dozen F-86's. The Air Force cleverly divided the MIG pilots into the "A" and "B" teams depending on their relative skills or more to the point if they were Russian (A) as opposed to Chinese or Korean (B). The MIG-15 more or less corresponded to the Luftwaffe Heinkel HE-178 that was first tested in 1939. To further entangle matters the first MIG recovered after a shootdown had a British made Rolls-Royce jet engine. It then became known that Britain sold fifteen jet engines to the Soviets.

An Air Force Security Service detachment based on an island off the coast of North Korea routinely monitored ground to MIG Pilot voice communications in Russian. The Soviet unit was identified as the crack "Guards Air Regiment" from the Moscow environs.

ASA units intercepted traffic from an Air Defense organization that stretched across North Korea and reported and tracked air attacks irrespective of which American Service was involved. The messages were in a simple code that kept me busy in breaking its variations that changed every few days. In a deviation from the standard Soviet style radio call signs of three letters or numbers (CX4, A8G etc.) this network used the names of flowers in the Korean Language to identify each other during transmissions. This indicated a possible correlation with vocal call signs that would be used in voice transmissions between radar units, anti-aircraft batteries and pilots aloft.

Departing from the standard security bureaucratic policy of "compartmentalization", I was authorized to go up "on the roof" to our now permanent intercept facility constructed atop the Headquarters building. I referred to it as my walk among the flowers.

Bypassing the procedure in the normal flow of intercepted messages, I would sit next to the operators assigned to copy this Air Defense network and observe the text to see if the key had changed. If it had, I would have a few hours jump on the reduction of the new key. This was one of the few remaining "tactical" sources of intelligence that emanated from Tokyo. The translated results were immediately flashed to the appropriate Air Force or Navy commands. In essence it would be a daily update on the whereabouts and magnitudes of the North Korean "Flak Alleys".

This Air Defense organization was composed of units that possessed mobile 120-millimeter radar controlled anti-aircraft weapons. These were up-to-date and formidably arrayed around major cities and transportation hubs. The North Korean Air Defense also worked in conjunction with Railway Supply units for mobility and ammunition. Railway Supply used primitive encryption systems that were easily broken and rarely changed. The commander of Railway Supply and his communications center was aboard a train, protected by anti-aircraft weapons aboard flatcars that hid from daily daytime air attack in railway tunnels. It was a cat and mouse game to track his whereabouts and try to eliminate his headquarters. We never got him.

The U. S. Navy mounted a major air offensive against strategic and logistics targets in the Eastern areas of North Korea. Unfortunately they were using slow carrier based World War II generation "Corsairs" that were no match for radar controlled 120 MM artillery. At least one aircraft a day was being shot out of the sky. The carrier based jet-aircraft as well as F-86's kept a respectable altitude around the "Flak Alleys".

One of the few roundabout acknowledgments of the key role communications intelligence played in the Korean War was hinted at in the 1954 movie "The Bridges at Toko-ri", based on the novel by James Michener. In the last scene of the movie when the Naval aircraft carrier commander played by Frederick March was informed that the downed Pilot William Holden and the helicopter pilot played by Mickey Rooney were both killed in North Korea, it was authenticated by "Army Intelligence". Someone "in the know" about the North Korean Air Defense intercepts by ASA leaked this information. The Air Defense network routinely transmitted the pilot's name and type of aircraft that they had shot down. The aircraft commander's name was usually emblazoned on the fuselage below the canopy.

The "strategic" air attack by both American services on North Korea was a failure. The railroads were rarely out of action, easily repaired and the road transportation became efficient. The Chinese forces approached 500,000 well-supplied men including artillery and tank units. The North Koreans were also completely re-supplied and were able to construct and mount air operations out of Air Bases throughout North Korea.

In October 1951 the military situation was at a stalemate and the intelligence from the enemy's combat communications was drying up. The use of unbreakable encryption - "the one-time pad" was slowly proliferating throughout the NKPA command structure. The principle North Korean cryptographic network - between Supreme Headquarters in Pyongyang, it's forward equivalent and each Army Corps was now unreadable with the subsequent loss of the most valuable intelligence about the enemy's capabilities and intentions.

Furthermore, traffic analysis was inadequate as the NKPA and the Chinese Communist Forces (CCF) were connecting their units by wire - landlines; either voice, telegraphic or teleprinter. Intercept volume, particularly lower echelon decipherable messages, dropped considerably.

Conversely, Headquarters - Army Security Agency Pacific was growing by leaps and bounds. It had become rank heavy - Majors and Light Colonels were being assigned to the company and it was necessary to provide bureaucratic "commands" for these officers. New sections, divisions and departments were set up. Our cryptanalysis section was moved from the modern headquarters building to the second floor of an older wooden structure above the IBM tabulating machine section. We made way for a huge table containing a three-dimensional relief map of Korea, complete with acetate overlays with the locations of military units penciled in. It was pure "eye-wash" to impress visiting VIP's, but serving no real function whatsoever with a West-Point Lt. Colonel in charge.

What was once a small headquarters company with administrative details handled by captains, warrant officers and non-coms was now structured as a regiment with "S" sections; S-1 Personnel, S-2 Security, S-3 Operations and S-4 Logistics (formerly supply) with each "commanded" by field-grade officers who had no intelligence experience. We joked that if the entire company was on a march there would be Captains and Majors for "Road-Guards". As the size of the organization grew the productivity of valuable intelligence declined, due more to the tightened communications security of the enemy.

An Army-wide reorganization of Army Security Agency was underway. In Korea, within the Eighth Army, the 60th SSC (Signal Service Company) was re-designated the 320th CRC (Communications Reconnaissance Company). Communications Reconnaissance Battalions were established, with additional CRC's that reported "their product" to the parallel Army Corps and Divisional structure. All functioned under a Comm Recon Group that reported to Eighth Army Headquarters. It was a massive and expensive organization complete with intercept, direction finding, traffic analysis, code breaking and translation staffs, with very little intelligence available to provide. It was too late, justified by the reputation for invaluable intelligence provided by the "ad-Hoc" rag-tag arrangements of the first year of the Korean War.--

Jack LaDove upon his promotion to sergeant.
The First Tokyo Arsenal is in the background. –

As a result of being "Rank-Heavy" and the influx of high-ranking sergeants, promotions were very scarce for both officers and enlisted men - those doing the most productive work. If one finagled a transfer to a newly created section it usually entailed a promotion - it was inappropriate for a field grade officer to have low ranking enlisted men to command. It was a childish and petty situation, harking back to a pre-war Army that created severe morale problems.

Dick Copeland and myself openly discussed transferring out, but we were just as openly informed that we would remain in cryptanalysis in Tokyo until our enlistment's terminated. Technically we were actually "draftees", as all enlistments were extended one year by presidential executive order. This blanket involuntary servitude did not sit very well with the troops, especially without any compensation or precise justification.

Among the sparse NKPA daily intercepts a new system appeared. Just a few messages, that looked to me as easily decipherable were handed to me by Sgt. Dugan. I took them over to Copeland's desk and said to him "Take a crack at it. It may be the last breakable system of the War and you would have something to tell your grandchildren". Cope handed them back to me and said "No, it is all yours, John".

The simple system was a newly created NKPA Artillery Supply network that was supporting autonomous artillery battalions, Chinese as well as North Korean. The enemy was obviously planning a long war of attrition. The revitalized NKPA was now a formidable foe, supported by extensive artillery and occupying most of the locations along the line as the Chinese pulled a short distance back. Eighth army, lacking high-level COMINT and facing forceful firepower engaged in futile attacks such as those at the ridges aptly named "Heartbreak" and "Bloody". This set the pattern for the remainder of the war, sacrificing expendable American lives for Korean real estate of dubious military value.

After going through the futility of applying for a transfer either within or out of Army Security Agency, Cope and I decided to force the issue and go AWOL - that is take a few unauthorized days off. Accordingly, one day at lunchtime after announcing our intentions at the office, we went to the PX, exchanged dollars for yen and headed for the hills by train.

Two days later, at high noon we returned to the post. The company commander immediately tried to separate us and apply company punishment, that is a slap on the wrist. I asked if we had made the morning report as army regulations required. The Japanese assistant company clerk replied that we had. We then stated that we are exercising our right to a court martial, where we could plead our case to a non-ASA officer. We forfeited our "Liberty" passes and were restricted to the post as expected.

A week later we were informed that we were to receive legal advice from the Judge Advocates office in GHQ at 1300 hours in the Finance building in downtown Tokyo. We presented ourselves at the proper place and time and Cope was called in first. He emerged from the Major officer's office five minutes later and made the motion towards me of his corporal's stripes coming off. He had been court-martialed.

It was my turn. I explained our rationale for demanding a military trial in order to facilitate a transfer. Luckily I had copies of citations that I had received that I presented to the Major. I also called to his attention the fact that we both had recently been awarded the Good Conduct Medal.

He said "Call your buddy back in". Cope re-entered and the Major asked us to sit down. We chatted for a few moments and he finally stated that he was legally bound to enforce military discipline, which we expected – a twenty-five dollar fine, reduction to grade E-2, private, and no confinement. He wished us the best of luck and stated that felt he was interviewing applicants for Officer's Candidate School rather than conducting a summary court's martial.

Cope had a small penknife and with it we removed our corporal's stripes on the way back to the post. We went to the first sergeant and informed him of the results of the court martial and requested the return our class "A" pass. And while he was at it would he please obtain for us our authentic metallic good conduct medals, which we were awarded on August 31st. The old soldier, who was well aware of what we were up to, asked us with good nature if we stayed up nights thinking of things to torment him with. We received the medals a few days later.

At about four o'clock we then returned to our desks in operations and just sat there. Technical Sgt. Francis Dugan brought some traffic over and handed it to me. I stated "I could not touch it, as according to Army Regulation, SR-380-160-10 an enlisted man must be grade E-3, that is PFC or higher to handle information classified TOP SECRET. Furthermore, although those intercepted messages are only classified SECRET, if I scribbled in just one Korean syllable it would turn into TOP SECRET-code word. Nothing personal, Frank, I just would not want to get anyone in trouble for violating security regulations".

He sort of agreed and took the messages over to Lt. Toft's desk as she was the only officer present, and conferred with her. She called me over to a corner of the office and with tears in her eyes asked why Richard and I were doing this. She said we could confide in her. She had such high hopes for us if we stayed in the Agency and went back to Washington. I related all we wanted was a transfer out. If we didn't get it the easy way, we now had nothing further to lose if we tried other methods. I asserted that her boss, Capt. Ligon, has succeeded in driving out of the section any capable people including Jack LaDove and Jim McCloy. Now it was our turn. She threw up her hands and said she didn't know what to do. Cope and I spent the rest of the day thumbing through some Korean study material and dictionaries. We thought we would be Korea bound shortly and after boning-up, could qualify as translators.

The next morning upon arriving at our desks, Capt. Ligon hissed at us that Colonel Greiner had authorized a waiver of the security regulations and we were ordered to return to work decoding North Korean messages. There was precious little left to decrypt, that any other available technician could easily have handled.

Several days later we were called to the post adjutant's office. Major McMillan's called Cope and I in, he sat us down and wanted to know the real story. We simply said, "we wanted out". He anticipated our complaint about lack of promotions and said something was being done about it. Cope retorted that everyone who transferred out of the section, and remained within the Agency, was immediately promoted. The Major said he would look into this as he appeared to be sincere.

Furthermore, Major McMillan knew about the incompetent officers by saying they were just putting in their nine-to-five day and something will also be done about that too, such as transfer to Korea. I stated that it was not just appearing day-to-day, but dereliction of duty, destruction of valuable intelligence documents and malfeasance in office that only an Inspector General's or Congressional investigation could resolve.

Cope chimed in that he was thinking of writing to his Senator Margaret Chase Smith of Maine. The Major visibly looked startled at these statements. I added that due to security regulations we could not go into further detail and that I was confident that there would some day be a congressional investigation, similar to the "Pearl Harbor" inquiry.

He turned dramatic and informed me that I had a decoration, the Bronze Star that he had never received in his entire army career. Finally, aware that we both had about nine months remaining in our Army service, in a military-academy-command tone he orated "You men will leave here Sergeants". This ended the session, was blatant bribery and meant that there would be no transfers.

Having no further alternatives, Cope and I took the relatively drastic step of requesting for "personal reasons" revocation of our Cryptologic Clearance. This option, similar to the offense AWOL (acronym for "absent without official leave"), having no civilian equivalent, did not involve criminal intent or moral turpitude and could be easily explained.

Within a week we were removed from duty. We were stripped of our MOS (Military Occupation Specialty) 3808 - Cryptanalysis Technician and awarded that of Basic Soldier - 0007. Cope shipped out first. After a debriefing by the S-2 (security) officer, he was transferred to Camp Drake replacement center, and subsequently assigned to a medical supply depot in central Japan.

I did not receive a security debriefing, but had a notation placed on my service record that under security regulations I was not to be assigned to an army unit where "danger to capture" exists. At the replacement center at Camp Drake, the officers responsible for reassignment, possibly never seeing such an entry before concluded that I was a "Sole Survivor". Being a sole surviving member of a family was strictly enforced in the military services for preventing a situation that may jeopardize life or limb. This was a result of the Navy's "Five Sullivan Brothers" being killed in a single action during World War II.

Accordingly, I was re-awarded my MOS - 3808 and along with several other "sole survivors" was flown to Okinawa and assigned to a Signal Corps unit where I became night manager of a small telephone exchange. I was happily back in the "Real Army" - where normal foul-ups occur. I was promoted for the third time to PFC two months later, but they misspelled my name on the orders. In April 1952 I was on an Army Transport cruising across the Pacific to be honorably discharged.

---The author, Jack LaDove and Gene Scarborough at the reunion of the 60th SSC in 1992 at Portland, Oregon.---

Epilogue

All three of us were discharged in the spring of 1952. Dick Copeland, after attending the University of Maine for a while, re-enlisted in the U. S. Air Force, switched to the Coast Guard, attained the rank of Warrant Officer, put in a full twenty years, married and had three children before retiring at home in Rockland, Maine.

Jack LaDove became an Engineering Design Consultant, left his native Cleveland for San Francisco, married and had two children. In his retirement he founded the ASAPAC reunion group, whose membership awarded him the lifetime title of Grand Bazook.

As for myself, I majored in mathematics-statistics at the University of Wyoming, then returned to New York and signed on with IBM to program the first commercially available computers. After leaving IBM in 1958 I became one of the first of many "Computer Programming Consultants" that continues to the present. This could well be the subject of another book in the works - "The Ancient History of Computers". In between computers I found time to marry and raise five beautiful actresses, some of whom get paid for it. In addition there are four grandsons.

Reunions

In 1987 under the guidance of Don Woods the 60th Signal Service Company had its first reunion in Tacoma, Washington. Organized along the lines of a Veteran's of Foreign Wars (VFW) post the membership elected Jim McCloy as the first commander. It has held many successful and enjoyable annual reunions since then. The 16th will be held in Syracuse, New York in September of 2002.

--- Jim McCloy, then and now, in Tokyo 1951 and at a reunion of the 60th SSC with compatriots---

The 60th SSC held a reunion in 1992 in Portland, Oregon attended by Gene Scarborough, Youn P. Kim, Jim McCloy and myself. Jack LaDove attended by invitation and under the counsel of Don Woods used the 60th as a template to start an ASAPAC alumni group. In 1993, at the Drawbridge Inn in Covington, Kentucky just outside of Cincinnati, ASAPAC's first reunion was held overlapping with the 60th SSC. ASAPAC's 2002 reunion the tenth will be at the same place.

Both Don Woods and Jack LaDove put in many long hours tracking down long lost former members of each unit, sadly over sixty percent having passed on. The current active membership of the 60th and ASAPAC annual reunion groups is roughly the same - just over a hundred and fifty active attendees, including spouses, girl friends and family. Both units have a mailing list of over 300 veterans, with about a forty percent cross membership. Many pleasant annual reunions have been held throughout the country, along with friends, spouses and descendants of the members. Long forgotten situations, that were once highly classified, can now be recalled, openly discussed and laughed at.---

---The Grand Bazook, Youn P. Kim, Gene Scarborough and the author at Portland, Oregon in 1992---

Security lapses and penetrations

There were three definitely known penetrations of the communications intelligence establishment over the last fifty years or so.

Foremost and most publicized of course were the British "Cambridge Five" led by Kim Philby. Philby was alleged to have been looking over the ASA civilian cryptanalyst Gardner's shoulder as he decrypted the Soviet VENONA espionage messages that implicated the Rosenbergs and others in the plot to steal the secrets of the atomic bomb. There is almost as much disinformation as actual facts on the VENONA project floating about. Most of the "breaks" into the encryption systems did not occur until the mid-nineteen-fifties when the first real computers were available to use as a "brute-force" attack on the material. The VENONA translations released have the actual dates of decryption/translation missing as well as details of which particular Soviet system was used. Actually, "who knew what when" can never be established, leaving the field open to any interpretation.

A not so well known security penetration was that of William Weisband. He had been at Arlington Hall for many years as a Russian translator and was assumed to have also tipped-off the Soviets to the VENONA unraveling of their espionage network's ciphers. Additionally, he was also aware of other Russian military codebreaking attainments and was in a position in 1950 to be knowledgeable about similar North Korean cryptanalytic results. He was never tried for espionage, but merely had his wrist slapped for refusing to testify before a grand jury.

The well-publicized defections of NSA technicians William Martin and Bernon Mitchell in 1960 to the Soviet Union enabled the Russians to get a bird's eye view of American cryptology. Due to "compartmentalization" their access to intelligence information was limited, but internal gossip gleaned during their careers in the Navy Security Group in Japan as well as in NSA at Ft. Meade no doubt contained interesting tid-bits of data about our intelligence efforts against North Korea.

Not well recognized would be the name of the Canadian Herbert Norman who tragically committed suicide just as he was appointed Canadian ambassador to Egypt. The jury on this man is still out and may never be reconvened. If he were a Soviet spy, and that is a very big if, he would have been well positioned in the Canadian Embassy as the head of the liaison mission to the allied occupation of Japan from 1946 to 1950. He was also on General MacArthur's GHQ counter-intelligence staff as the head of the Research and Analysis Branch in 1945. During World War II he was very actively engaged in the Canadian communication's intelligence effort. He was employed as a translator of Japanese messages in the "National Research Council Examination Unit", also known as the "Communications Security Establishment". One of the first questions he would have sought an answer to when the Korean War broke out was how successful were the Americans in solving North Korean encryption systems. Then, if he knew what would he have done with the answer?

Closer to home or rather ASAPAC, two sergeants who shall remain unknown, were transferred out of Army Security Agency in 1951 by having their Cryptologic/Top Secret clearances removed. They committed the unpardonable sin of appearing at a party at a Japanese home where the guests included several important members of the Japanese Communist party. No doubt the guest list also included some undercover counter intelligence corps (CIC) operatives. Both men had access to top-secret intelligence information and were trained cryptanalysis technicians, but worked in Tokyo at different specialties. Whether or not they were passing information to their party friends will probably never be known. It is still up to them.

In 1968 the communications intelligence ship "Pueblo" was boarded at sea by North Koreans and forced into Wonsan harbor. Neither NSA nor the U. S. Navy has ever given the American public a full accounting of the damage done to the COMINT effort. American cryptographic security was catastrophically impaired by the capture of high-level encryption machines which was revealed by the Soviets. The Walker family spy ring supplied the necessary software.

Others penetrations of security include among others the known spies; Petersen, Pollard, the FBI disaster Hanssen, and the CIA's Aldrich Ames. Again, the people of the United States are in the dark as to the extent of the damage done to "national security" in any of these cases.

__________Declassification Campaign__________

All relevant correspondence will be found in Appendix D. it is a chronology of the efforts of the National Security Agency to prevent the publication of this book. As well as the revelation that its personnel will use the secrecy statutes and executive orders to conceal dereliction of duty and malfeasance in office.

Phase I - Review of this book. On April 20, 1991 I started to get serious about writing this account. A letter was submitted to Senator Moynihan of New York inquiring as to which was the proper government authority to review the text and pass judgment on whether or not the material was still classified. In September of 1991 the Senator's office forwarded to me a letter from the Office of Assistant Secretary of Defense, Defense Security Programs, that outlined the current declassification procedures as well as the proper office for submission of manuscripts for review.

Consequently, in January 1992 a three-page extract from this book of a single incident concerning the Korean War was submitted. The manuscript embraced several items; the existence of pre-war North Korean communications, the decryption after the commencement of hostilities; the failure to translate the material and inform higher headquarters.

In a little over a month a terse letter was sent by the Chief, Directorate for Freedom of Information and Security Review, Office of the Assistant Secretary of Defense stating that the National Security Agency has advised that the information in the manuscript is still classified.

An appeal to the Information Security Oversight Office was immediately composed and sent inferring that the classification by NSA was done to preclude embarrassment to that agency and its predecessors. In August of 1992 a reply was received from the Director of that office, Steven Garfinkel, indicating that an independent review of NSA's decision determined that although the events occurred over thirty-five years ago disclosure could reasonably be expected to cause SERIOUS damage to the national security. The last citation was taken word-for-word from the text of Executive Order 12356, except that the adjective "serious" was interjected. I felt that the classification was unwarranted and brought the matter to the attention of Senator Alfonse D'Amato of New York who was on the Senate Intelligence Committee. That went nowhere.

Upon my relocation to New Jersey, in November of 1992 the matter was then addressed to Senator Bill Bradley of that state. He sympathized with the general public's displeasure with the atmosphere of secrecy that still pervaded government information since the end of the "Cold War" and further suggested that the matter should be couched in a Freedom of Information Act request.

Phase II - Freedom of Information Act. A FOIA request was sent to the National Security Agency in March of 1993 that asked for any information relating to "Messages from the North Korean People's Army .. up to the start of hostilities on June 25, 1950 ". The request was summarily denied on June 11th stipulating that an appeal may be filed with that agency within sixty days. A response to the appeal would be given within twenty days upon receipt. This was done on August 9th.

No response was received. After several futile telephone calls, on December 27th an unpleasant letter was sent to the Director of NSA Admiral John McConnell, with copies to Senator Bill Bradley and Congressman Dick Zimmer of New Jersey.

Finally on the 18th of March 1994 a letter was received from William P. Crowell of NSA's Freedom of Information/Privacy Act Appeals Authority. The gist of this note was ".. A careful review ..a through search was done... I have determined that no inventories of the type you requested exist and no responsive records were found". On June 25th 2000, NSA's Cryptologic Museum released a brief history commemorating the fiftieth anniversary of the Korean War. It stated that there were over 200 pre-war North Korean Army messages.

Phase III - Second Freedom of Information Act Request. The so-called "Brownell Report" was the result of an investigation initiated by President Harry Truman to assess America's communications intelligence program with emphasis on the failures associated with the Korean War. The net result of the report was the creation by executive order of the National Security Agency on November 4, 1952. The order is still classified, although a summary account can be found in the library of the President Harry S. Truman museum in Missouri.

A partially declassified "Brownell Report" was summarized and published by the Aegean Park Press in 1980 under the title "The Origins of the National Security Agency". One interesting comment associated with the conditions at Arlington Hall during the Korean War stated "The officers in charge often appear greatly inferior in skill and experience to the civilian professionals under their command...". Nothing in the report mentioned any messages from North Korea that were intercepted before the start of the war. Therefore, on February of 1996 another FOIA request was submitted to NSA requesting an "unredacted" copy of the Brownell report along with other documents.

In December of that year a demand for seventy-five dollars was received from NSA to cover the cost of researching the "Brownell Report". On January 1st of 1997 a postal money order for that amount was dispatched along with a note expressing hope that this would expedite matters. Immediately on the 7th a letter was received expressing insult that the term "expedite" was used.

Mr. Daniel E. Barchanowicz, Chief - FOIA/PA Branch evidently, like all civil servants throughout the world, construe the term "expedite" when associated with money to connote "bribery to get something done". I replied with a letter explaining how the rest of world and most dictionaries define the term expedite. Ms. Barbara

Paisley as the new "Chief" replaced Mr. Barchanowicz. She was courteous, yet pessimistic as to when the report would be forthcoming after several telephone calls.

Needless to say nothing "got done" until December 2001. There was numerous letters back and fourth, as well as over thirty telephone calls on my part. The final document received was still heavily "redacted" (censored) and was no different from the original release of the same in 1980. Two sample pages from the report are in the appendix indicating that the number of radio intercept positions in 1950 is still classified. However, only with the intervention by Congressman Rush Holt of New Jersey I did have my $75 refunded.

President William Clinton promulgated executive order #12958 that covers classified information on April 17, 1995. It was to take effect in six months and stated that all classified information over twenty five years old will be automatically declassified. However, there was a five-year grace period in which any agency could review documents and pass judgment as to whether or not there was a loophole through which they could avoid declassifying. An amended executive order #13142 extended the grace period to six and a half years when intelligence information or more than two federal agencies are involved.

There is no reason whatsoever, either of a technical intelligence nature ("sources and methods") or involving a foreign sovereignty (the late Great Britain), why the "Brownell Report" should still remain virtually completely classified. Unless, of course, the investigation was faulty and failed to take into consideration, or had never been appraised of the existence of North Korean communications prior to the attack. Even at this late date the American people deserve full disclosure.

Appendix A: Military documents.

GENERAL HEADQUARTERS
FAR EAST COMMAND

CITATION FOR THE BRONZE STAR MEDAL

Corporal JOHN E. MILMORE, RA12303399 (then Private First Class), Signal Corps, United States Army, distinguished himself by meritorious service with Operations Section, Headquarters, Army Security Agency, Pacific, General Headquarters, Far East Command, from 27 June to 2 November 1950. Despite the lack of previous experience, Corporal MILMORE, through unusual initiative and conscientious efforts, produced invaluable intelligence information. In his work on a top secret project, he displayed remarkable brilliance and aptitude in his field of endeavor and he greatly aided all units in the field in gathering and processing information. Corporal MILMORE's sustained devotion to duty, and significant achievements contributed materially to the intelligence mission in support of the United Nations' campaign against aggression in Korea, reflecting credit on himself and the military service.

Received July 28, 1951.

GENERAL HEADQUARTERS
FAR EAST COMMAND

GENERAL ORDERS)
:
NO.........186)

APO 500
18 July 1951

	Section
Distinguished-Service Cross - - Award......	I
Legion of Merit - - Awards.................	II
Bronze Star Medal - - Awards...............	III
Bronze Star Medal (Oak-Leaf Cluster) - - Award..................................	IV
Commendation Ribbon with Metal Pendant - - Award..................................	V

I. AWARD OF THE DISTINGUISHED-SERVICE CROSS. By direction of the President, under the provisions of the act of Congress approved 9 July 1918 (WD Bul 43, 1918), and pursuant to authority contained in AR 600-45 and Department of the Army radiogram, 10 July 1950, the Distinguished-Service Cross for extraordinary heroism in action is awarded to the following-named officer:

Major EARLE H. JORDAN, Jr., O129360O (then Captain), Infantry, United States Army, Commanding Officer, Company M, 3d Battalion, 31st Infantry Regiment, distinguished himself by extraordinary heroism in action against an armed enemy of the United Nations near the Chosin Reservoir, Korea, from 28 November to 2 December 1950. The 3d Battalion, in defensive positions for the night, was surrounded,and ferociously attacked at approximately 0500 hours on 28 November by a numerically superior hostile force, seriously penetrating the outer line of resistance, inflicting heavy casualties and causing a disorderly withdrawal of troops from the east side of the perimeter. Realizing the gravity of the situation, Major JORDAN, despite intense mortar, automatic weapons, small arms and grenade fire, rallied and reorganized the withdrawing troops and personally supervised the establishment of a new perimeter. During the ensuing two days he fearlessly led his command against repeated attacks and constantly braved withering machine gun and mortar fire to move among his men, encouraging and deploying them to insure maximum defense for each position. Upon orders to withdraw, Major JORDAN supervised the evacuation of the wounded and, while directing the retrograde action of his unit, two road blocks were encountered by the motor convoy. Major JORDAN immediately rallied, organized and led determined attacks against well-entrenched positions on high ground, routing the ruthless foe from their strongpoints and enabling the convoy to resume its march. Although seriously wounded, Major JORDAN held his forces together and, dominating and controlling the critical situation through sheer force of his heroic example, led the command to successful completion of the mission. Major JORDAN's inspirational leadership, unflinching courage and intrepid actions reflect utmost credit on himself and the honored traditions of the military service. Entered Federal service from Maine. (This award supersedes the award of the Silver Star to Major Jordan, for gallantry in action during the same period, published in General Orders 227, Headquarters, 7th Infantry Division, 1951.)

Page 1.

II. AWARD OF THE LEGION OF MERIT. By direction of the President, under the provisions of the act of Congress approved 20 July 1942 (sec III, WD Bul 40, 1942) and Executive Order 9260, 29 October 1942 (sec I, WD Bul 54, 1942), and pursuant to authority contained in Department of the Army radiogram, 10 July 1950, the Legion of Merit for exceptionally meritorious conduct in the performance of outstanding service during the periods indicated is awarded to the following-named officers:

Major CHARLES R. ALBRIGHT, 036502 (then Captain), Signal Corps, United States Army, 28 August to 2 November 1950. Entered Federal service from Oklahoma. (This award supersedes the award of the Bronze Star Medal to Major Albright, published in General Orders 91, Headquarters, X Corps, 1951.)

Lieutenant Colonel IRWIN A. EDWARDS, 032149 (then Major), General Staff Corps, United States Army, 16 September to 2 November 1950. Entered Federal service from Oklahoma. (This award supersedes the award of the Bronze Star Medal (Second Bronze Oak-Leaf Cluster) to Lieutenant Colonel Edwards, published in General Orders 85, Headquarters, 7th Infantry Division, 1950.)

III. AWARD OF THE BRONZE STAR MEDAL. By direction of the President, under the provisions of Executive Order 9419, 4 February 1944 (sec II, WD Bul 3, 1944), and pursuant to authority contained in AR 600-45 and Department of the Army radiogram, 10 July 1950, the Bronze Star Medal for meritorious service in connection with military operations against an enemy of the United Nations during the periods indicated is awarded to the following-named officers and enlisted man:

Lieutenant Colonel VERNER C. AURELL, 0154911, Signal Corps, United States Army, 27 June to 2 November 1950. Entered Federal service from Virginia.

Major CHESTER A. BAKER, 0373526, General Staff Corps, United States Army, 9 September to 2 November 1950. Entered Federal service from Kansas.

Corporal JOHN E. MILMORE, RA 12303399 (then Private First Class), Signal Corps, United States Army, 27 June to 2 November 1950. Entered Federal service from New York.

Major LEON T. SCARBROUGH, 01165949, Artillery, United States Army, 10 July 1950 to 28 February 1951. Entered Federal service from North Carolina.

Lieutenant Colonel JOHN J. TOMAN, 0359426, Artillery, United States Army, 25 June to 2 November 1950. Entered Federal service from Wisconsin.

IV. AWARD OF THE BRONZE STAR MEDAL (OAK-LEAF CLUSTER). By direction of the President, under the provisions of Executive Order 9419, 4 February 1944 (sec II, WD Bul 3, 1944), and pursuant to authority contained in AR 600-45 and Department of the Army radiogram, 10 July 1950, the Bronze Star Medal (First Bronze Oak-Leaf Cluster) for meritorious service in connection with military operations against an enemy of the United Nations during the period indicated is awarded to the following-named officer:

Major ORVILLE E. BLOCH, 032736, Infantry, United States Army, 27 June 1950 to 9 March 1951. Entered Federal service from North Dakota.

V. AWARD OF THE COMMENDATION RIBBON WITH METAL PENDANT. By direction of the Secretary of the Army, and pursuant to authority contained in AR 600-45 and Department of the Army radiogram, 10 July 1950, the Commendation Ribbon with Metal Pendant for meritorious service during the period indicated is awarded to the following-named enlisted man:

Sergeant First Class CORNELIUS P. McNALLY, RA 39250719, Finance Department, United States Army, 25 June to 2 November 1950. Entered Federal service from North Dakota.

AG 200.6

BY COMMAND OF GENERAL RIDGWAY:

DOYLE O. HICKEY
Lieutenant General, General Staff Corps
Chief of Staff

OFFICIAL:

K. B. BUSH
Brigadier General, USA
Adjutant General

GENERAL HEADQUARTERS
FAR EAST COMMAND

☆ ☆ ☆ ☆ ☆ ☆ ☆ ☆ ☆ ☆ ☆ ☆ ☆ ☆ ☆

THIS

CERTIFICATE of ACHIEVEMENT

IS PRESENTED TO

Corporal John E. Milmore, RA12303399, Headquarters, Army Security Agency, Pacific, 8621st Administrative Area Unit, APO 500

CITATION

For outstanding performance of duty with Operations Branch, Headquarters, Army Security Agency, Pacific, during the period 25 June to 23 December 1950. By his diligent attention to duty and his untiring efforts he produced results in difficult assignments that have contributed immeasurably to the success of the mission of the Army Security Agency.

Edwin C. Greiner

EDWIN C. GREINER
Colonel, Armor
Chief, ASA, Pacific

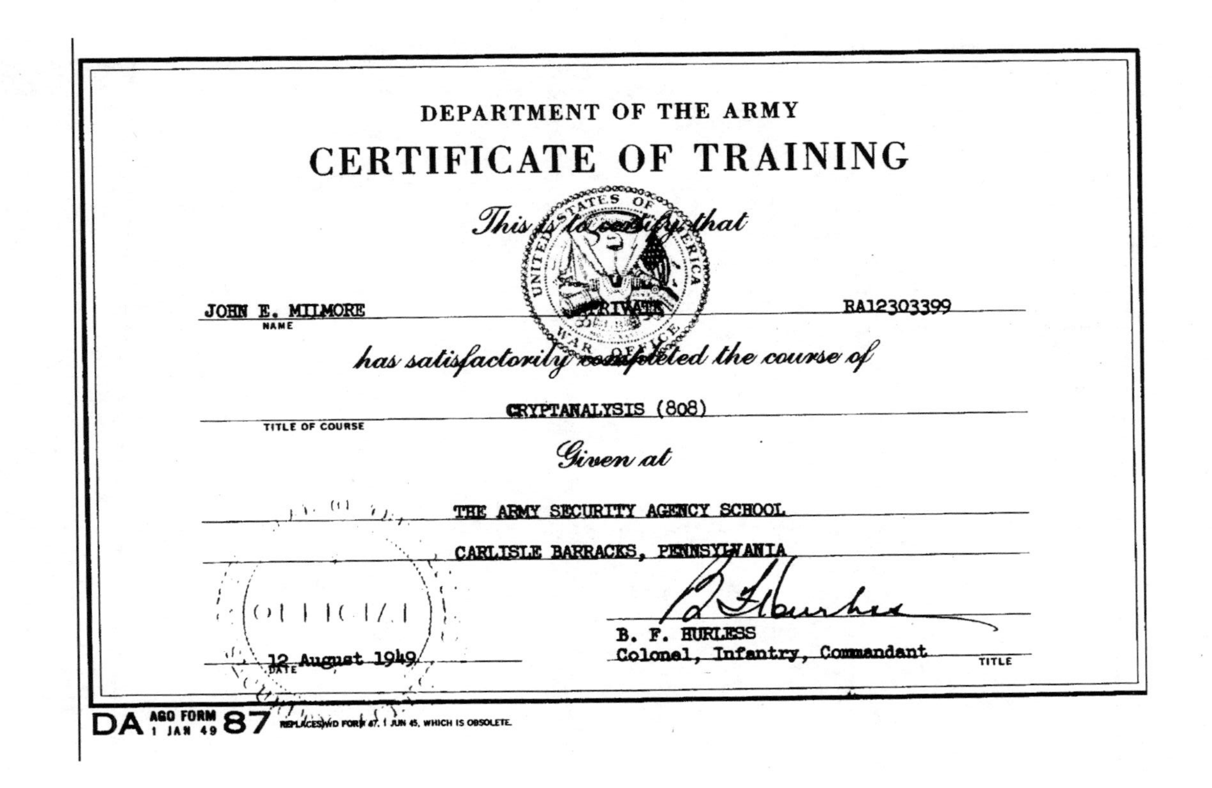

DEPARTMENT OF THE ARMY

CERTIFICATE OF TRAINING

This is to certify that

JOHN E. MILMORE — PRIVATE — RA12303399

NAME

has satisfactorily completed the course of

CRYPTANALYSIS (808)

TITLE OF COURSE

Given at

THE ARMY SECURITY AGENCY SCHOOL

CARLISLE BARRACKS, PENNSYLVANIA

12 August 1949

DATE

B. F. HURLESS

Colonel, Infantry, Commandant

TITLE

DA AGO FORM 87 1 JAN 49 REPLACES WD FORM 87, 1 JUN 45, WHICH IS OBSOLETE.

English	Pronunciation	Korean Spelling
digging trenches	*CH*AHM-haw-rool PAH-noon choong	참호를파는중
laying mines	CHEER-er POO-sul choong	지뢰를부설중
preparing an airfield	PEE-hang CHAHNG-ool TAHNG-noon choong	비행장을닦는중
laying in supplies	KOON-bip-hoo-mool NAL-in-oon choong	비품을내리는중
repairing equipment	KOON-bip-hoom SOO-sun choong	군비품수선중
building tank traps	"tank" HAHM-jung-ool NAWN-noon choong	탱크함정을놓는중
Which direction did they go?	koo-P'YUNG-jung-dool UN-oo JAW-goo-raw kahss-SOOM-nik-gah?	그병정들어느쪽으로갔습니가?
Show us where they are	UD-ee-dool IN-noon-jee CHAWM KAH-rooch-huh CHOO-see-yaw	어데를있는지좀가르쳐주시요

8. LETTERS, NUMBERS, SIZE, TIME, ETC.

NAMES OF THE LETTERS

Letter	Name as Pronounced	Letter	Name as Pronounced
ㅏ	AH	ㅟ	WEE
ㅑ	YAH	ㅞ	WAY
ㅓ	UH	ㄱ	KEE-uk *or* KAH
ㅕ	YUH	ㄴ	NEE-oon *or* NAH
ㅗ	AW	ㄷ	TEE-goot *or* TAH
ㅛ	YAW	ㄹ	NEE-ool *or* LAH
ㅜ	OO	ㅁ	MEE-oom *or* MAH
ㅠ	YOO	ㅂ	PEE-oop *or* PAH
ㅡ	OO	ㅅ	SEE-awt *or* SAH
ㅣ	EE	ㅇ	HANG *or* AH
ㅔ	A	ㅈ	CHEE-oot *or* CHAH
ㅢ	ER	ㅊ	*CH*EE-oot *or* *CH*AH
ㅘ	WAH	ㅋ	*K*EE-hoot *or* *K*AH
ㅝ	WUH		

Letter	Name as Pronounced	Letter	Name as Pronounced
ㅌ	TEE-hoot *or* TAH	ㄸ	DAH
ㅍ	PEE-oop *or* PAH	ㅃ	BAH
ㅎ	HEE-hoot *or* HAH	ㅆ	SAH
ㄲ	GAH	ㅉ	JAH

AMOUNT

English	*Pronunciation*	*Korean Spelling*
A few	KUJ-uh M'YUK-ga	그저 몇 개
Several *or* Many	MAH-ah-nee	많이
Not many *or* Little	CHAW-gawm	조금
Very much	PUK MAH-ah-nee	퍽 많이

NUMBER SYSTEMS

There are two sets of number words in Korean. One, the native Korean system, goes up through ninety-nine only; the other, a system borrowed from Chinese, goes on up higher. When these number words are joined to other words for purposes of counting, there are changes and irregularities. Therefore in this section are listed not only the numbers themselves, but some of the more important combinations.

THE CHINESE NUMBERS

Nos.	*Pronunciation*	*Korean Spelling*	*Nos.*	*Pronunciation*	*Korean Spelling*	*Nos.*	*Pronunciation*	*Korean Spelling*
1	IL	일	11	SIB-il	십일	10	SIP	십
2	EE	이	12	SIB-ee	십이	20	EE-sip	이십
3	SAHM	삼	13	SIP-sahm	십삼	30	SAHM-sip	삼십
4	SAH	사	14	SIP-sah	십사	40	SAH-sip	사십
5	AW	오	15	SIB-aw	십오	50	AW-sip	오십
6	YOOK	육	16	SIM-n'yook	십육	60	YOOK-sip	육십
7	*CH*IL	칠				70	*CH*IL-sip	칠십
8	*P*AHL	팔	17	SIP-*ch*il	십칠	80	*P*AHL-sip	팔십
9	KOO	구	18	SIP-hahl	십팔	90	KOO-sip	구십
10	SIP	십	19	SIP-goo	십구			
100	PAK	백						
1,000	*CH*UN	천						
0,000	MAHN	만						

The words for "twenty-seven," "thirty-nine," etc. are made just as in English. Thus "twenty-seven" is "EE-sip *CH*IL."

Army Security Agency School

GUIDE

CARLISLE BARRACKS
PENNSYLVANIA

Appendix A. ASA School Course Requirements.

PREREQUISITES FOR COURSES

OFFICERS COURSE — GENERAL, PART I:

Regular Army or Category III. General Service (Physical Profile). CRYPTOGRAPHIC CLEARANCE. Age: 21-35 years. 2d Lt. to Captain. High School graduate. Experience in civilian; Mathematics, Chemistry, Language, Radio, or Electrical Engineering, or Commercial Communications, (Desirable but not mandatory). Experience Military; Signal Communication, Signal Intelligence, or Communication Security, desirable but not mandatory. Waivers, —for mandatory qualifications, may be granted by the Chief, Army Security Agency, in meritorious cases, or for cogent military reasons.

The Military Occupation Code (MOS) specialties for the enlisted men's courses below are as follows:

799 - Morse code Radio Interceptor.
1799 – Non-Morse Radio Interceptor.
868 – Interception Equipment Maintenance.
801 - Cryptographic Equipment Maintenance.
709 - Traffic Analyst (Radio).
807 – Code Compiler and Cryptosecurity Specialist.
808 – Cryptanalysis Technician (Code Breaker).

Note that all enlisted courses require an AGCT score of 110 or above. This is roughly equivalent to an IQ score. Officers up to Lt. Colonel must be High School graduates.

OFFICERS COURSE — GENERAL, PART II

Graduate of Part I. Regular Army or Category III. General Service (Physical profile). CRYPTOGRAPHIC CLEARANCE. Age: 24-40 years. Grade: 1st Lt. to Lt. Col. High School graduate. Same for civilian as above. Military experience: Signal Communication, Signal Intelligence, or Signal Communication Security is mandatory. The experience to be on the Division level or equivalent in command or staff capacity, is desirable. Same waivers as above.

799 COURSE (ENLISTED MEN)

AGCT of 110 or higher. ARC-1 of 110 or higher, or SCCA of 55 or higher. Or if below the standards above, has had previous schooling or experience which indicates an ability to satisfactorily complete the course. CRYPTOGRAPHIC CLEARANCE.

1799 COURSE (ENLISTED MEN)

AGCT of 110 or higher. High mechanical and electrical aptitude. CRYPTOGRAPHIC CLEARANCE mandatory. Must be a 766 or previous equivalent experience. Must have some background in electricity, either scholastically or professionally, or have some previous communications experience. Training as 799 or 542 desirable.

868 COURSE (ENLISTED MEN)

AGCT of 110 or higher. CRYPTOGRAPHIC CLEARANCE, mandatory. Must be a 648 or 649, or possess previous civilian or military experience equivalent thereto.

801 C-1 COURSE (ENLISTED MEN)

AGCT of 110 or higher. CRYPTOGRAPHIC CLEARANCE, mandatory. Must be a 239, or equivalent.

801 C-2 COURSE (ENLISTED MEN)

AGCT of 110 or higher. CRYPTOGRAPHIC CLEARANCE, mandatory. MOS of 239 or equivalent experience or education desirable. Must have high mechanical and electrical aptitudes.

709 COURSE (ENLISTED MEN)

AGCT of 110 or higher. ASA-1 Test score of 90 or higher. High school graduate. Expressed interest in related subjects (crossword puzzles, chess, mathematical problems, etc.). Able to meet standards for cryptographic clearance. Training in language, mathematics, science or radio theory preferred but not mandatory.

807 COURSE (ENLISTED MEN)

Same as 709.

808 COURSE (ENLISTED MEN)

Same as 709.

ARMY SECURITY AGENCY SCHOOL

Certificate of Completion of Subcourse

This is to certify, That Pvt. John E. Milmore, Signal Corps,

"A" Branch, ASA School, Carlisle Barracks, Pennsylvania has successfully
(Address)

completed Subcourse No. 20-16, Military Cryptanalysis, Part II
(Title of Subcourse)

Extension Course of the Army Security Agency School (1948-1949 Announcement) with a

rating of Superior credit 100.

Date 11 August, 1949.

Charles W. Kelley
CHARLES W. KELLEY
Instructor, Extension Training Division

APPROVED:

BY ORDER OF THE COMMANDANT:

Carl E. McProud
Act'g Director, Extension Training Division
CARL E. MCPROUD
1st Lt FA

Restricted

WAR DEPARTMENT
OFFICE OF THE CHIEF SIGNAL OFFICER
WASHINGTON

MILITARY CRYPTANALYSIS

Part I

MONOALPHABETIC SUBSTITUTION SYSTEMS

By

WILLIAM F. FRIEDMAN
Principal Cryptanalyst
Chief of Signal Intelligence Section
War Plans and Training Division

PREPARED UNDER THE DIRECTION OF THE
CHIEF SIGNAL OFFICER

UNITED STATES
GOVERNMENT PRINTING OFFICE
WASHINGTON : 1938

MILITARY CRYPTANALYSIS. PART III. SIMPLER VARIETIES OF APERIODIC SUBSTITUTION SYSTEMS

CONTENTS

(III)

The entire series Military Cryptanalysis parts I, II, III and IV are available from the Agean Park Press.

GENERAL HEADQUARTERS
FAR EAST COMMAND
APO 500

1 May 51

AG 201 - Milmore, John E AGOM

LO 121-3

SUBJECT: Detached Service

TO: EM concerned, ASAPAC APO 500

1. CPL JOHN E MILMORE RA12303399 WP o/a 4 May 51 to 60th Sig Svc Co, APO 301 on DS for an indefinite period in connection with Army Security Agency activities. Upon compl or when sooner relieved by proper auth will return to proper station.

2. Tvl by mil acft, rail and govt mtr transportation auth. TDN. An alws of sixty-five (65) pounds personal baggage auth while tvlg by air. No per diem auth.

3. EM is auth access to cryptologic information UP SR 380-160-10.

4. EM may draw currently auth clothing and equipment for tvl to Korea. All clothing and equipment issued will be returned within seventy-two (72) hours after compl of DS.

5. Immunizations and physical inspection as prescribed by Cir 9, FEC 27 Feb 50 will be completed prior to departure.

BY COMMAND OF LIEUTENANT GENERAL RIDGWAY:

Thomas F. Whaley
THOMAS F. WHALEY
Captain, AGC
Asst Adj Gen

DISTRIBUTION:
Chief ASAPAC APO 500 (15)
Cpl Milmore (15) thru ASAPAC APO 500
CO, 60th Sig Svc Co, APO 301 (1)

"Decipherment - translation of the above Military Order"

GENERAL HEADQUARTERS
FAR EAST COMMAND

[The primary military command unit of the U. S. Army's forces in the pacific area, West of Hawaii. Formerly General MacArthur's, also loosely includes Navy and Air Force]

APO [Army Post Office] 500 [the mailing address for the sometimes mobile military unit now located in Tokyo, Japan, but serviced from San Francisco]
AG 201 [An enlisted man's permanent record file that stays with the administrator at his/hers permanent assignment].
AGOM [unknown, probably an Adjutant General abbreviation]
LO 121-3 [Presumably, logistics order with priority level]
SUBJECT: Detached Service [Standard military heading, Detached Service; implies temporary assignment to another unit, sometimes abbreviated to TDY or temporary duty
TO: [Also standard salutation], EM [Enlisted man] concerned, ASAPAC [Army Security Agency Pacific] APO 500 [See above]

1. CPL [Corporal] JOHN E MILMORE RA [Regular Army] 12303399 [Unique individual serial Number] WP [Will proceed] o/a [on or about] 4 May 51 to 60th Sig Svc Co [60th Signal Service Company, the ASA's mobile radio intelligence unit], APO 301 [See above, postal unit 301 also out of San Francisco, but now located in Korea] on DS [Detached Service] for an indefinite period in connection with Army Security Agency activities. Upon compl [completion] or sooner relieved by proper auth [Authority] will return to proper station.
2. Tvl by mil acft, [Travel by military aircraft] rail and govt mtr [government motor] transportation auth [in this case it means authorized]. TDN [Travel deemed necessary]. An alws [allowance] of sixty-five (65) pounds personal baggage auth [authorized] while tvlg [traveling] by air. No per diem auth [No daily money authorized or advanced for meals or other expenses].

3. EM [The enlisted man is auth [authorized] access to cryptologic information UP SR [Under the Provisions of Special Regulation] 380-160-10. [the 380 series of regulations cover who will have access to the euphemistic cover term - cryptologic for TOP SECRET code word intelligence information].
4. EM [The enlisted man may draw currently auth [authorized] clothing and equipment for tvl [travel] to Korea. [mainly this was a rifle and a steel helmet. If it was winter, heavy duty boots and a parka would have been in order]. All clothing and equipment issued will be returned within seventy-two (72) hours after compl of DS. [completion of Detached Service, a remarkably clear sentence].
5. Immunizations and physical inspection as prescribed by Cir [Circular] 9, FEC 27 Feb 50 [Far East Command, dated 27 February 27th, 1950] will be completed prior to departure. [That is if certain immunizations were not current, they should be brought up to date. This included typhus, typhoid, encephalitis and tetanus. Physical inspection is Army "nice talk" for determination by a doctor to see if a venereal disease is present. Also known as "Short Arm" inspection. This was not performed.]

BY COMMAND OF LIEUTENANT GENERAL
RIDGWAY:
[the ultimate authority in military leadership of this organization, the Far East Command].

/ signed /

THOMAS F. WHALEY
Captain, AGC [Adjutant General Corps]
Asst Adj Gen [Assistant Adjutant General]

DISTRIBUTION:
Who gets how many copies of this order]

Chief ASAPAC [no, not an American Indian leader but the commanding officer of Army Security Agency Pacific, Colonel Edwin C. Greiner] APO 500 (15) [fifteen copies]

Cpl [Corporal] Milmore (15) thru ASAPAC APO 500

CO [Commanding Officer, at the time Captain Don Mulvey],

60th Sig Svc Co, APO 301 (1) [see above].

Thousands of similar, stereotypic orders were issued daily within the Far East Command and other military units. As you can see from the above, quantities such as hours and pounds are repeated in parenthesis. Such standard practice is necessary to avoid misinterpretation and confusion. However, it presents a code breaker with ample opportunities if this order was encrypted and transmitted by interceptable means. The American Army's standardized approach in correspondence did not differ much from their North Korean adversary's usage.

Appendix B: Bibliography-----

Walker enjoyed another advantage: excellent communications intelligence (COMINT) from breaking some encoded NKPA radio transmissions. The full details of this operation remain classified, but a little background and a cursory outline of successes in Korea can be pieced together from unclassified material.

During World War II the Allied forces had benefited greatly from breaking German and Japanese military and diplomatic codes. In the postwar years Washington had directed code-breaking efforts against the Soviet Union and other Communist nations, but owing to a lack of funding, a shortage of qualified and highly motivated code breakers and linguists, bureaucratic inertia, infighting and other factors, it had not been able to duplicate the remarkable COMINT successes of World War II. Most encoded radio traffic out of Moscow was unbreakable.[16]

As a result of the effort directed toward Moscow and elsewhere, North Korean codes had of necessity been grossly neglected. A study conducted in June 1952 by George A. Brownell and others (the so-called Brownell Report) revealed that the State Department and Pentagon had ranked North Korea near the bottom (twelfth or lower) on its postwar code-breaking priority list. Hence, by the time the Korean War began almost nothing noteworthy had been achieved, and, Brownell reported, Washington had been "poorly prepared to handle Korean traffic."[17]

The upshot was that unlike the Army commanders of World War II, Johnnie Walker had no flow of decoded "strategic" enemy radio traffic from Washington to assist him. What he got, he had to acquire locally—"tactical" COMINT. In this effort, however, Walker's G-2 section was remarkably, even astoundingly, successful. One reason, a senior G-2 officer wrote, was that the NKPA was careless and had an "obvious lack of communications security." As a result, Eighth Army cryptographic specialists were able to "break into" the NKPA "tactical radio network" and "read" NKPA traffic. "They had a 'pad' which they changed weekly," a G-2 specialist explained. "It took only one day to break it, then we could read NKPA traffic for four or five days running." As a result of this tactical code breaking, plus the usual battlefield intelligence, the Eighth Army G-2 specialist wrote, "throughout July and August, every major enemy attack was known in advance. . . ."[18]

Possessing this advance knowledge proved to be a priceless asset for Walker. Alerted to enemy moves in advance, he was able to shift his few reserves within the Pusan Perimeter to key spots at the key times, further capitalizing on his favorable "interior lines of communication." Inasmuch as COMINT was ultra top secret and every effort was made to limit its distribution and conceal its output, only a handful of personnel in Eighth Army were aware of it. Those not "in the picture" would unwittingly praise

Page 171, "Korea - The Forgotten War", By Clay Blair (1987)

Walker for his seemingly uncanny—or even magical—ability to divine enemy intentions.

Without a doubt the best book written about the Korean War is "The Forgotten War – America in Korea 1950-1953" by Clay Blair. Doubleday 1987. Unfortunately the information printed above concerning COMINT at Mr. Blair's disposal admittedly came from "over the transom' – unofficial sources. The above extract is slightly inaccurate in that there were no ASA units in Korea prior to September 1950. All code breaking was performed in Tokyo at ASAPAC. The code breaking success cited above reflected the cryptographic situation in the spring of 1951 rather than that of the summer of 1950.

There are many other books including the "Official" Army histories. All are devoid of any reference to COMINT code breaking or radio intelligence therefore none are worth mentioning. The sole exception is the political indictment by I. F. Stone "The Hidden History of the Korean War 1950-1951" – Preface edition 1988 by Bruce Cumings. Originally written in 1952 there is speculation that someday a declassification of communications intelligence with reference to the Korean War would shed light on the subject. Disappointingly there is nothing available from the American side but, there is possibilities from the South Korean, British (from their intercept station in Hong Kong) or the forces of Chiang Kai- Shek on Taiwan.

Two books of interest about intelligence are "The U.S. Intelligence Community" by Jeffrey T. Richelson, Ballinger Publishing 1989 and "Senseless Secrets – The Failures of U. S. Military Intelligence, From George Washington to the Present" by Lt. Col. (Ret.) Michael Lee Lanning – Birch Lane Press 1996. The first is a very good overview of alphabet soup of U. S. Intelligence agencies as well as the security laws and regulations that surround them. The second is written as an evaluation from the viewpoint of the ultimate user of intelligence.

There are only three books exclusively about the National Security Agency. The first is "The Origin and Development of the National Security Agency" from the Aegean Park Press - 1981. It is an abstract of the "Brownell Report" which is a still highly classified investigation conducted in 1952 by a joint committee of the departments of Defense and State. The Aegean Park Press specializes in books about cryptology and those interested are well advised to obtain their catalogue – P.O. Box 2120 Walnut Creek, CA 94595 or [books@aegeanparkpress.com]. The other books are James Bamford's "The Puzzle Palace" which was superseded by "The Body of Secrets: anatomy of the ultra-secret National Security Agency: from the Cold War through the dawn of a new century" – Doubleday 2001. Both are directly concerned with NSA. The "Puzzle Palace" (Houghton Mifflin Company 1982) unfortunately was full of statements such as "might be", "must be" or "could have been" which reflected the speculative nature of Mr. Bamford's research. The second book with the blessing of NSA's public affairs office resembles more of a "public relations puff-piece" rather than responsible investigative reporting. He got it all wrong about the Korean War, but then he could only relate what NSA wanted him to report. Both are still well worth reading with that caveat.

The foremost book on cryptography is certainly "The Codebreakers – The Story of Secret Writing" by David Kahn. Macmillan Company, New York – 1967. The book is the quintessential treatise on cryptography. I am acquainted with David and we have had several pleasant meetings. At those times security considerations prevented me from relating to him the full story of cryptography and the Korean War. I hope that a future revision of "The Codebreakers" will include information from "#1 Code Break Boy".

All other books of this genre, about a dozen, are concerned mostly with World War II, particularly from the British viewpoint. Some titles are "Secret and Urgent" - Fletcher Pratt.

Blue Ribbon Books, Garden City, N. Y. 1942. Written in 1939 and probably out of print but a light reading introduction to cryptography.

Others include "The Broken Seal" - L. Farago, "MacArthur's ULTRA" - E. Drea, "Double-Edged Secrets" – Holmes, "Top Secret Ultra" - P. Calvocoressi, "The Code Breakers" - Hinsley and Stripp, "Station X" – Smith, "The Story of Magic" - Rowlett. An excellent biography of the grand daddy of American cryptography is "The Man Who Broke Purple – The Life of Colonel William F. Friedman, Who Deciphered the Japanese Code in World War II" by R. Clark Little, Brown & Co. 1977. Another readable British horn blower is "The Sigint Secrets – The Signals Intelligence War 1900 to Today" Nigel West, Morrow & Co. 1986.

The National Security Agency (NSA) through their Cryptologic Museum at Fort Meade, Maryland has produced five papers On Communications Intelligence (COMINT or SIGINT) during and prior to the Korean War. Some are available on NSA's website [www.nsa.gov]. The largest is admittedly hurried and "cobbled together". All attempt to exonerate the civilian agency AFSA from lack of effective performance - AFSA the predecessor of NSA.

The largest is by Hatch & Benson. From various unspecified sources including oral histories. Contains many errors, but does mention over two hundred pre-war North Korean military messages. States that a "retrospective" analysis of the traffic in 1952 indicated nothing that would tip-off the attack on June 25th 1950. The reply to my freedom of information request in 1994 said that no such traffic existed. There was a message that I personally decrypted and translated that was passed on June 22nd that indicated an attack on Oi Jung Bu.

Another by Jill Frahm cites reports by AFSA (Armed Forces Security Agency, the predecessor of NSA) called "AFSA Semi-Monthly Report for the Office of Operations" the paper is inconsistent as well as inaccurate. Tries to "whitewash" the conflict between AFSA and ASAPAC (Army Security Agency Pacific) as to who actually produced the intelligence that aided the defense and breakout from the "Pusan Perimeter". It was all ASAPAC, except for civilian AFSA translators who were dispatched to Tokyo, such as Norman Wild, Erskine St. Clair and others. The "Korean" typewriter praised in the article was an absolute failure. Another by Patrick D. Weadon is a worthless rehash of the above two. Contains a significant typo – states that American soldiers to insure the security of their communications used the M-204. It should be M-209 as indicated in the photograph. It was not a secure system; Jim McCloy broke it during maneuvers out of Vint Hill station.

One archival report is by Thomas R. Johnson. A "Redacted" (Heavy black scribbles) formerly TOP SECRET UMBRA undated document. Principally Air Force public relations oriented again little mention of the dominant role ASAPAC played in the Korean War. Another is an extract from the "Cryptologic Quarterly", also undated and redacted. Leans heavily on British GCHQ - Government Communications Headquarters, a euphemism for British communications intelligence.

An Independently produced monograph by Matthew M. Aid. More accurate and critical then any of the above, with a few errors. Has the Chief ASAPAC Col. Rubin going to GHQ-FEC in September, instead of late July 1950. Also insultingly states that the enlisted "Conscripts" (we were all Regular Army – RA) were undisciplined alcoholics and suffering from venereal diseases. Didn't address the Officer's behavior or those relieved of their commands. Cites FOIA requested information – ASAPAC and 60th Signal Service Company annual and semi-annual reports. Reports that others have been unable to obtain. Officers having scant knowledge of cryptology or communications intelligence produced these official reports particularly in the 60th Signal Service Company in the first year of the war. The commanding officers Captains Flaherty and Mulvey were nice guys and competent leaders but COMINT lightweights. There were no cryptanalytic officers present and the translators were much to busy to write reports.

The two-part article was published under "British Auspices" therefore a requisite was blaming Generals MacArthur and Willoughby for everything that went wrong. Doesn't mention that intercept assignments were micro managed from Washington by either AFSA or the pentagon's general staff. Furthermore, it sidesteps the Soviet spies that infiltrated the American intelligence communities such as the alleged Canadian agent Osborn and the notorious English Cambridge five- Philby, Maclean and others.

Clay Blair's one page summary in "Korea – the forgotten War" is still the best.

Appendix C: Cryptographic Technicalities.---

A page from a declassified, captured Russian code book. Probably used by the 3rd Long Range Bomber Army. Two "lend-Lease" items were the aircraft for code groups 069 (Catalina) and 081 (C-47). Code group 077 was the PO-2 or the polyichov bi-plane, or known to us as "bed-check Charlie".

015 ЗАПАДН...
016 МЕТЕЛЬ
018 МОРЕ...балл,а/ов
020 МОРОСЬ
021 ОБЛАЧНОСТЬ
023 ОБЛАЧНОСТЬ...балл,а/ов
024 ОСАДКИ
026 ПОЗЕМКА
028 ПУРГА
029 СЛОИСТО-ДОЖДЕВ,ая/ые
030 СЛОИСТО-КУЧЕВ,ая/ые
031 СЕВЕРО-ВОСТОЧНЫЙ
033 СЕВЕРО-ЗАПАДНЫЙ
035 СЕВЕР,ный
036 СНЕГОПАД
040 ТЕПЛЫЙ ФРОНТ
060 ЮГО-ЗАПАДНЫЙ
062 ЯСНО

САМОЛЕТЫ

063 АМФИБИЯ
065 А-20ж
067 ИЛ-2
068 ИЛ-10
069 КАТАЛИНА
071 ЛИ-2
072 ЛА-5
073 ЛА-7
075 ПЕ-2
077 ПО-2
079 С-2
081 СИ-47
082 ТУ-2

Russian Three-Digit Air Force Code.

Комплект № 0|22

017	778	019	848	843	337	877	968	332	022	875
026	287	588	864	257	516	134	091	760	340	788
031	655	173	742	233	251	880	732	037	025	684
045	844	682	965	983	502	467	826	906	658	681
063	817	175	243	776	053	104	151	450	709	521
094	220	856	448	054	702	855	627	140	091	921
107	338	756	580	844	121	372	180	558	879	808
125	893	930	030	257	557	575	783	451	704	252
132	454	003	372	209	154	877	852	290	470	039
147	061	313	208	248	744	686	325	335	776	607
158	485	135	422	702	474	213	047	901	479	111
160	321	337	708	917	550	430	326	182	825	786
208	464	163	104	474	674	455	032	921	281	438
216	145	207	207	431	581	272	082	433	600	660
229	667	667	053	266	741	594	225	202	481	164

Declassified Russian three-digit additive. Probably captured by the German Army during World War II.

Plain text letter:

ㄱ	ㄴ	ㄷ	ㄹ	ㅁ	ㅂ	ㅅ	ㅇ	ㅈ	ㅊ	ㅋ	ㅌ	ㅍ	ㅎ	ㅏ	ㅑ	ㅓ	ㅕ	ㅗ	ㅛ	ㅜ	ㅠ	ㅡ	ㅣ
01	02	03	04	05	06	07	08	09	10	11	12	13	14	15	16	17	18	19	20	21	22	23	24

Cipher Equivalent:

___North Korean Air Force Encryption System (June 1950)_______
This simple enciphering system was the first cryptanalysis of many during during the Korean War. The North Korean Air Force used it for over a year.

This was the #1 of thirty-seven different North Korean Military cryptographic systems that I successfully cryptanalyzed during the first year of the Korean War. It was the same generic system used by Julius Caesar as well as the 1930's and forties radio characters Dick Tracy, Orphan Annie and Captain Midnight – either with a "secret decoder" ring or badge. I don't know which one the NKPA used.

Letter	Cipher Equivalent			
ㄱ	01	26	51	76
ㄴ	02	27	52	77
ㄷ	03	28	53	78
ㄹ	04	29	54	79
ㅁ	05	30	55	80
ㅂ	06	31	56	81
ㅅ	07	32	57	82
ㅇ	08	33	58	83
ㅈ	09	34	59	84
ㅊ	10	35	60	85
ㅋ	11	36	61	86
ㅌ	12	37	62	87
ㅍ	13	38	63	88
ㅎ	14	39	64	89
ㅏ	15	40	65	90
ㅑ	16	41	66	91
ㅓ	17	42	67	92
ㅕ	18	43	68	93
ㅗ	19	44	69	94
ㅛ	20	45	70	95
ㅜ	21	46	71	96
ㅠ	22	47	72	97
ㅡ	23	48	73	98
ㅣ	24	49	74	99
period.	25	50	75	00

NKPA Constabulary Encryption System (Nov. 1950)

	0	1	2	3	4	5	6	7
-	ㄱ	ㄴ	ㄷ	ㄹ	ㅁ	ㅂ	ㅅ	ㅇ
8	ㅈ	ㅊ	ㅋ	ㅌ	ㅍ	ㅎ	ㅏ	ㅑ
9	ㅓ	ㅕ	ㅗ	ㅛ	ㅜ	ㅠ	ㅡ	ㅣ

The letters in the top row are encoded by the single digits above them. The second and third rows use two digits, the 8 or 9 at the left plus the digit above.

This typical Soviet espionage enciphering system was the kind used by the NKPA political security agents during the Korean War. Sometimes referred to by the Russians as a "monome-dinome" or by the Americans as a "straddling checkerboard" substitution system. Encrypted messages were further subjected to a transposition methodology which greatly enhanced the security of the system. For example the syllables of the phrase "Long live comrade Kim Il Sung" would be encoded as follows:
김 일 성 동 지 만 세 = 0974 7973 6867 2927 8097 4861 66897.
The thirty digits would then be written into a simple rectangle and then transcribed out by a prearranged key.

key: 3 4 2 5 1 6

0 9 7 4 7 9
7 3 6 8 6 7
2 9 2 7 8 0
0 9 7 4 8 6
1 6 7 8 9 7

The columns of the rectangle are removed according to the key sequence yielding the message:
76889 76277 07201 93996 48748 97067

The reverse procedure would decipher the message.

In practice the letters are arranged with the most frequently used letters in the top row of the "checkerboard", usually from an easily remembered word. The transposition key can also be derived from a word or phrase. Instead of a simple rectangle a more irregular geometric figure is used. It is a practically unbreakable system.

7 4 6 3 1 2 5
조 선 인 민 군 만 세

이 일 얀 대 장 동 지
앞 미 국 병 정 들 전
진 하 는 길 입 듸 가
삼 사 단 대 령 리 백

A unique encryption system used by the NKPA in August 1951. A message to the commander of the 21st regiment from a Colonel in the third division is written, then the Korean syllables are transposed in the alphabetic sequence of the key phrase "Long live the Korean Peoples's Army". The key phrase is included in the final message as follows:

군 장 정 입 령 만 동 들 듸 리 민 대

병 길 대 선 일 미 하 사 세 지 잔 가

백 인 얀 국 는 단 조 이 앞 진 삼

Statistics of the Letters of the Korean Language

Letter	Total %	As Initial	As Final	approximate transliteration
				Consonants (14)
ㄱ	.0553	.0418	.0136	K or G
ㄴ	.0824	.0239	.0585	N
ㄷ	.0339	.0339	-	T or D
ㄹ	.0689	.0228	.0460	L
ㅁ	.0268	.0196	.0071	M
ㅂ	.0268	.0125	.0143	P or B
ㅅ	.0564	.0435	.0128	S
ㅇ	.1200	.0872	.0328	silent, "ng" as final
ㅈ	.0253	.0246	.0007	J or Ch (hard)
ㅊ	.0061	.0057	.0004	Ch (soft)
ㅋ	.0029	.0029	-	K (soft)
ㅌ	.0103	.0096	.0007	T (soft)
ㅍ	.0143	.0139	.0004	P (soft)
ㅎ	.0400	.0385	.0014	H
				Vowels (10)
ㅏ	.1071	.1017	.0054	A
ㅑ	.0014	.0014	-	Ya
ㅓ	.0535	.0510	.0025	U
ㅕ	.0136	.0136	-	Yu
ㅗ	.0407	.0407	-	O
ㅛ	.0093	.0093	-	Yo
ㅜ	.0300	.0300	-	Oo
ㅠ	.0014	.0014	-	Yoo
ㅡ	.0685	.0685	-	Eu
ㅣ	.1053	.0567	.0485	I or ee

Relative frequencies of the letters of the Korean "Hangul" alphabet, expressed as a percentage. The initial frequencies of the consonants include the five doubled consonants. The final frequencies of the consonants also include any doubled consonants. The vowel final frequencies include the second or third letters of dipthongs or tripthongs. Source: 1,049 syllables of modern technical text.

TOP SECRET COPSE M1

New York-Moscow
1945
No. 25 (8 January)

To Victor [VIKTOR].

Your number 6047. Bass [BAS] received the Reef? [RIF"I] telegram 4 January. On 30 December Bass received a letter from the Bank [BANK] with the request to come by ¿himself?...... ....of the Reefs. Bass entrusted the business to a Carthaginian [KARFAGENSK"Y] lawyer, who on 4 January advised by telephone that the Reefs question was being examined by a special commission of the Bank. As soon as the letter from the Bank had been received we asked Bass to check on whether the visa had been issued[;] he, however, has not yet done this, wishing beforehand to find out from the lawyer how the business is going. So far there is no ¿documentary evidence? that the visa has not been issued, but the examination of the business by the commission ....entrance visa had [has?] not been issued. We......Bass to leave for Carthage [KARFAGEN] on 9 January and jointly with the lawyer get more precise information about the question and if the visa has not yet been issued to ¿spend?? as much time as is required on this. Inasmuch as at the end of......Marcus [MARKUS] advised Bass that the visa had been issued we have just asked Bass to get in touch with him immediately and get an explanation. Bass asked......to wait until the situation in Carthage was clarified on the grounds that Marcus's interference just now might definitively hamper the way the business is going. In a day or two upon Bass's return from Carthage we shall let you know a great deal about the situation.

19

May [MAY]

TOP SECRET COPSE

8 January

A sample of recently declassified translations of decryptions of Soviet Russian messages know as the "VENONA" release. The code word after the TOP SECRET Stamp is "COPSE". At that time (1950) it applied to intelligence obtained from successful cryptanalysis. It also sounded like the nickname for Richard Copeland, which we encouraged our Japanese friends to use, much to the consternation of those who were familiar with the term.

MATERIAL FROM "H" (1945)

From: WASHINGTON

To: MOSCOW

No: 1791

29 March 45

To the 8th Department.

Material from "H[G]"[i].

I am transmitting cipher telegram No. 95 of 8th March 1945 from the ISLAND's[ii] [OSTROVNOJ] Embassy in "SMYRNA[SMIRNA]"[iii] to the "POOL[OMUT]"[iv]:

"Sent to the Foreign Office [MID][v] as No. 714 and repeated to WASHINGTON.

1. [The remainder of the text (438 groups) has been largely recovered. It is a Russian translation of the telegram referred to above.]

[2 groups unrecoverable][a]

[1 group unrecoverable][a]

Note: [a] The WASHINGTON MGB officer's signature and reference number are unrecoverable.

Comment: [i] "H" : Abbreviation for HOMER, cover-name of Donald Duart MACLEAN. See Comment [i] in 3/NBF/T1725 issued 13th October, 1965.

[ii] ISLAND's: British.

[iii] SMYRNA : MOSCOW.

[iv] POOL : British Embassy in WASHINGTON.

[v] MID : Expansion MINISTERSTVO INOSTRANNYKh DEL.

Distribution:

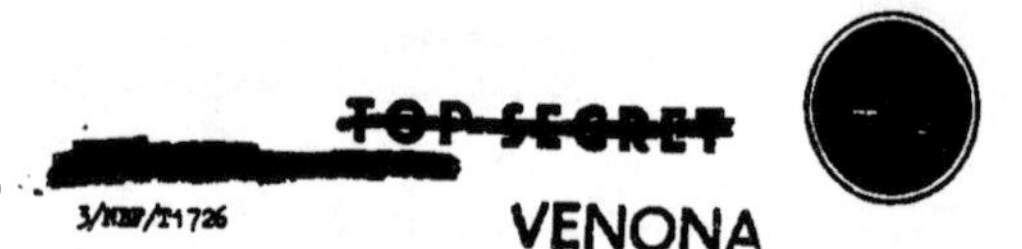

3/NBF/T1726

VENONA

193.

Another VENONA release. This one implicates the British spy Donald Maclean, who along with his compatriot Herbert "Kim" Philby no doubt relayed to their Russian controllers accounts of our codebreaking successes, causing the North Koreans to keep changing their encryption systems. Other VENONA messages clearly implicated the Rosenbergs - the notorious atomic bomb spies. The VENONA intercepts were still being worked on in the late 1970s.

V. THE BASIC SYSTEMS AS FOUND IN RUSSIAN CRYPTOGRAPHY

A. Substitution Systems

All the substitution systems found by the Germans in the cryptanalysis of Russian traffic are definitely code types. By code is meant not only a substitution system of considerable extent having arbitrary numerical or letter groups assigned as substitutes for the syllables, words and phrases of the language but also those substitution systems of small size which have values for elements in addition to single letters of the language, such as marks of punctuation, the 1-digit numbers and a few short words which are frequent in the traffic of the service for which the table is compiled. It may be noted in passing that the only case reported by the Germans of a true monoalphabetic substitution being used by the Russians, and that without re-encipherment, was between two radio operators in traffic concerned chiefly with women. Evidently it was a personal system being used without authority. These code systems varied in size from small signal tables with 100 groups or less to large books with 25,000 groups or more. They will be classified according to the lengths and types of code groups used in the substitution process, that is, into 2-figure, 3-figure, 2-figure-letter, etc. The original Russian designations will be indicated when known. Details of the various methods of re-encipherment that were used with these codes will be given under a separate heading.

1. 2-Figure Codes

Small signal tables comprising about 100 plain elements represented by 2-digit numbers were used by the Russians to encipher the operational traffic of the army and army airforce from regiment down to platoon during 1935 and until the change in organization of the RKKA which took place in 1942. The original RKKA designation was PT or chatter table. Signal tables of similar construction were used by the NKVD in the communications of their Frontier Troops and Coast Guard Units during the same period, but since the internal arrangements of the vocabularies of the NKVD tables (recovered by the Germans only through cryptanalysis) evidently could not be made to coincide with any of the basic arrangements of those captured in the "PT" series, it is likely that for NKVD usage there was another designation. The PT-35 (chatter table of year 1935) was in use from 1935 to 1939. PT-39 was used during period 1939-42; PT-41 during period 1941-45. PT-42 and PT-43 were also seen.

All these substitution tables, although differing in details of vocabulary, the use of variant readings and switch groups, conformed to the same general pattern. The 100 cells of a 10 by 10 square table were filled, sometimes in systematic order, sometimes in random order, with the 30 letters of the Russian alphabet, the 10 digits 0 to 9, the punctuation marks and the frequent words used in operational traffic. Along both the vertical and horizontal margins of this table the digits 0 to 9 were inscribed in random order as row and column coordinates. Encipherment of a particular word was accomplished by finding it within the substitution table and tracing orthogonally outwards from this cell to the row and column coordinates which were combined to give the 2-figure substitution. The enciphered messages were sent sometimes in

- 22 -

TOP SECRET SUEDE

---Typical Soviet cryptography as used by the North Koreans in 1950 and 1951. This information was gleaned from captured German Army sources. ---

An explanation of an additive key generation Methodology and the Solution. The use of the Fibonacci series expansion and its applications is well known in mathematics as well as in nature. In economics and investments the "Eliot Wave theory" is an example, while in biology it can be demonstrated in the growth of both snail shells and certain leaves. The standard Fibonacci sequence is represented by A + B = C, B + C = D, C + D = E and so on, results in the basic series 0 + 1 =1, 1 + 1 = 2, 1 + 2 = 3; that produces the sequence of sums as 0, 1, 2,

3, 5, 8, 13, 21, 34, 55, 89, 144,...and upwards. In cryptology there are several applications, both in "machine" encryption systems and in simple pencil-and-paper techniques. Numeric additive key generation used by the North Korean Peoples Army in 1951 is one that will now be explained.

The simple formula, using randomly selected A and B, produces A + B = C, then B + C = D, then C + D = E and so on that can be used for integers of any size to produce a long series of apparently random numbers subsequently used as an additive encryption key. Numbers of any magnitude can be used, but one distinction is necessary, that is whether or not "carrying" or "non-carrying" addition is used. In cryptography the use of "non-carrying" addition is the norm. Hence, for consistent usage among cryptographic personal it is the usual procedure. Example: 12345 added to 67890 would equal 79135, as opposed to the result 80235 if normal carrying addition were performed.

Regardless of which method is used the interaction of the unit's digit and the resulting array of digit sequences is always the same. In the above sample 5 + 0 = 5, then 0 + 5 = 5, then 5 + 5 = 0, and so on resulting in a sequence of 5 0 5 5 0 5 5 0 5 . . ., or the repetitive three digit sequence 5 0 5. It is obvious that the interaction of 0 + 0 would produce nothing but a sequence of zeros. The resulting sequences of the one hundred possible two digit combinations can be plotted yielding six distinct repetitive chains or sequences of digits. As noted above 0 + 0 would give a single digit chain of zero, any combination of 0 and 5 would give a three digit length of 5 0 5. The other combinations would be 2 and 6 a length of four [2 6 8 4, 2 6 8 4,..]; 1 and 3 a length of twelve, 0 and 2 a length of twenty and the longest 0 and 1 a length of sixty. All chain lengths are factors of sixty; therefore that is the maximum length of any units digit

Fibonacci expansion. The six possible digit streams are listed below. The lowest two-digit combination in the stream defines it.

0 + 0 = 0 Length = 1

0 + 1 = 1 2 3 5 8 3 1 4 5 9 4 3 7 0 7 7 4 1 5 6 1 7 8 5
3 8 1 9 0 9 9 8 7 5 2 7 9 6 5 1 6 7 3 0 3 3 6 9
5 4 9 3 2 5 7 2 9 1 0 1 Length = 60

0 + 2 = 2 4 6 0 6 6 2 8 0 8 8 6 4 0 4 4 8 2 0 2 Length = 20

0 + 5 = 5 0 5 Length = 3

1 + 3 = 4 7 1 8 9 7 6 3 9 2 1 3 Length = 12

2 + 6 = 8 4 2 6 Length = 4

The above sequences can be indexed to determine the position of any two-digit combination in its respective stream. Then the sequence can be extended in either direction. An example of an additive page from the "Crooked Line Cipher".

Column Numbers ______________>

line#	1	2	3	4	5	6	7	8	9	0
01	789	234	911	874	639	481	648	129	384	313
02	439	741	122	789	473	938	391	679	917	836
03	663	996	420	854	690	410	567	220	217	110
04	018	092	227	161	701	379	137	495	946	886
05	904	071	655	111	581	357	969	056	952	093
06	298	912	812	647	484	642	992	238	879	347
07	269	923	816	731	292	948	123	862	197	299
08	735	457	115	728	830	839	631	765	536	325
09	658	846	616	778	534	493	021	725	888	412
10	951	383	508	063	024	252	251	850	737	543
11	797	276	931	417	679	976	786	149	871	321
12	774	648	431	214	127	632	876	938	864	621

13	940	848	335	093	145	915	201	185	614	492
14	279	614	110	973	781	359	949	833	013	542
15	017	103	554	696	208	024	494	405	034	156
16	213	286	377	168	963	171	418	743	698	867
17	316	963	293	987	612	813	379	744	137	891
18	230	529	840	479	221	770	332	440	658	870
19	193	727	835	034	662	076	382	449	719	907
20	567	323	255	354	308	031	097	052	777	159
21	284	289	416	374	189	436	693	674	334	868
22	434	741	672	739	423	433	341	624	917	386
23	613	946	925	859	145	915	512	775	217	610
24	518	047	272	666	256	874	682	945	996	831
25	454	021	650	161	581	357	919	506	457	048
26	293	962	317	697	939	147	492	783	879	392
27	214	478	316	286	247	998	628	817	692	749
28	785	407	115	278	380	834	686	765	031	375
29	153	391	611	278	584	493	071	770	383	967
30	406	838	558	018	079	752	701	805	232	048
31	797	726	981	462	629	471	236	199	876	321
32	274	193	431	719	172	637	321	988	369	671
33	990	893	880	543	690	410	256	680	114	447
34	224	164	615	973	731	309	949	883	018	092
35	017	158	054	141	753	529	999	455	039	106
36	763	231	872	118	468	626	463	298	198	812
37	811	913	248	987	162	818	379	294	187	841
38	785	574	345	479	271	270	382	995	653	375
39	698	222	385	089	617	576	332	494	264	452
40	567	373	250	859	858	086	047	502	727	159
41	789	239	961	324	134	431	693	179	834	313
42	489	246	172	234	478	983	896	679	462	336
43	618	496	925	809	195	965	017	775	262	160
44	568	097	277	161	751	329	137	990	496	831
45	954	076	605	616	086	802	414	556	907	093
46	243	412	367	692	939	147	942	733	824	897

47	219	973	366	731	297	498	123	817	147	794
48	230	452	660	778	330	889	631	260	581	870
49	103	391	661	728	034	448	076	275	383	917
50	951	333	058	013	079	702	756	855	787	543

__In actual practice the NKPA used only 50 lines____

51	242	776	436	417	674	921	736	694	821	826
52	724	193	486	769	677	687	371	438	369	676
53	490	893	335	598	195	965	251	185	164	497
54	279	114	165	428	236	854	444	838	063	592
55	062	653	504	191	753	529	949	450	089	656
56	718	231	327	618	963	171	413	793	148	817
57	361	418	293	482	112	863	824	794	632	896
58	735	079	345	424	276	720	832	995	603	325
59	143	727	330	039	617	526	832	499	719	957
60	062	878	205	309	358	031	092	552	272	604

______From line 61 onwards the page repeats itself__

61	789	234	911	874	639	481	648	129	384	313
62	439	741	122	789	473	938	391	679	917	836
63	663	996	420	854	690	410	567	220	217	110

~~~

The above example is a generated additive page of ten three digit columns of a length of sixty rows similar to that used by the NKPA using non-carrying arithmetic. They employed a weak subterfuge of generating the sequences diagonally down the page in an alternating manner. The main diagonal starting in the position line one, column one is 789, 741, 420, 161, 581, 642, ... repeating at line 61. Note the unit's digit is the sequence 0+1 with a length of sixty, as is the sequence produced by the hundredth digit. The middle or tens digit chain has a length of four, that is the 2+6 or 2684, 2684. Starting on line one, column two, going down diagonally to the left
~~~

then reversing the direction is the sequence 234, 439, 663, 092, 655, 647, 292 and so on. The single digit chains of the units and tens digit are the 0+1 sequences of length sixty. The hundredths or first digit is the 0+2 cycle of length twenty.

In the first year of the war the North Koreans never changed their codebook or additive page at the same time. This would have presumably caused confusion in their communications. Consequently, when it was determined that a new page was in effect it was assumed that the underlying code had not changed. In breaking this system the approach was to position two or more messages "in depth", that is conjecture that their alignment resulted from their being encoded under the same segment of the additive page.

This could be done by noting the "hits" between messages, that is identical code groups that resulted from identical additive or by "differencing" - a methodology explained elsewhere. The more frequent attack was the assumption that certain NKPA Corps headquarters invariably started on the additive page at line one, position one. Additionally, some deputy corps commanders were garrulous and transmitted very long messages in excess of 500 groups, the length of the page. This meant that segments of the message were enciphered with the same additive key. Both events were violations of standard communications security practice, but a bountiful gift to a cryptanalyst.

Assuming stereotyped message beginnings or endings, once a break is made that yields twenty or more groups of coherent text the known six possible single digit chains can be entered and extended up and down a projected 500 group additive page. In no time at all entire messages would yield their additive keys. Once the proposed additive key failed to fulfill in sequence then the true top or bottom of the page had been reached.

The demonstrated example uses "non-carrying" addition. If normal addition is employed only the unit's digit is limited to a series length of sixty or less. The length of this repetitive cycle can be broken or interrupted by taking the high-order "carry-over" of the addition when it occurs, always a one, and adding it to the units digit. Other variations include using numbers of five digits in magnitude and only extracting the middle three for the additive. Additionally, if genuine transposition is introduced to scramble the digit streams it greatly expands the complexity of generation, but tends to approach the absolute security of true "one-time Pad".

The use of an alternating diagonal generation of the columns does not add any cryptographic strength to the system once the routine had been instituted. However, it must have provided a false sense of security to the users as they frequently heralded in their messages an upcoming change to the "crooked line" cipher system. The "Arlington Hall Dilettanti" dubbed the system "Boustrophedonic Fibonacci", but it could just as well have been entitled the "zigzag" method.

The system, if used properly, should have provided reasonable security. If message lengths were kept below 500 groups and if the starting position in the additive page was chosen at random then it would have been much more difficult to break into the system. Furthermore, if they had changed the additive page more frequently, as well as repaginate their operational code at the same time it would have been a significant setback in gathering intelligence. Please note in the example the fact that the propagated sequence repeated itself after sixty generations introducing a sum check to validate the arithmetic, as well as having the zigzagging columns also return to their original locations at the same time. This would insure that the complex generation technique was performed correctly.

The use of a master page of 500 random numbers, that was never used for encryption, to generate many additive pages provided a procedure to enable a military unit that was isolated and cut off logistically to continue to encode its communications. There would be 2,450 possible combinations of two 10-group strips to produce an additive page.

It was interesting to note that in the very early stages of the Korean War the NKPA used a small strip of twenty additive groups to encipher their messages. The use of such a small key was baffling to me at the time as it imparted very little security from cryptanalytic attack. Perhaps these were actually two strips of ten groups each that was the intended "seed" to produce the "one-time" additive pages that were used later in the conflict. Furthermore, it could have been that their cryptographers at the time were not fully trained in the more advanced techniques or the commanders along with their Russian advisers had not anticipated the need for sufficient communications security.

Appendix D:---

OFFICE OF THE ASSISTANT SECRETARY OF DEFENSE

WASHINGTON, DC 20301-3040

COMMAND, CONTROL, COMMUNICATIONS AND INTELLIGENCE

23 September 1991

Senator Daniel P. Moynihan
ATTN: Ms. Deborah A. Famighette
405 Lexington Avenue
41st Floor
New York, New York 10174

Dear Senator Moynihan:

This is in response to your letter of 25 June 1991 that forwarded correspondence from Mr. John Milmore expressing concern about the rigorous security restrictions that currently envelope the operations of the Federal Government and further requesting guidance on where he should submit a planned manuscript for security review.

In response to Mr. Milmore's concern about the length of time that documents remain classified, Executive Order 12356, "National Security Information," which prescribes a uniform system for classifying, declassifying, and safeguarding classified information throughout the Executive Branch, requires that information shall be classified as long as required by national security considerations, and when it can be determined, a specific date or event for declassification shall be set by the original classification authority.

Where cryptologic information is concerned, it is not possible to automatically declassify on a specific date or event. However, the following mechanisms do exist whereby classified National Security Agency (NSA) material must be reviewed for possible declassification and release to the public:

- The Freedom of Information Act (FOIA) allows a member of the public to request classified documents concerning a particular topic that could be declassified and released;
- The Mandatory Declassification Review provisions of Executive Order 12356 require that classified documents be reviewed for possible declassification if requested by a member of the public; and
- All classified cryptologic material that is at least 50 years old must be systematically reviewed by NSA for possible declassification in accordance with the Information Security Oversight Office (ISOO) Directive No. 1 that implements Executive Order 12356.

In response to Mr. Milmore's request for guidance, he should submit his manuscript to the Office of the Assistant Secretary of Defense (Public Affairs) (OASD(PA)) for review since he indicated that he was a former U.S. Army cryptanalyst. If warranted, OASD(PA) can refer relevant sections to NSA.

As requested, a copy of this response is enclosed along with Mr. Milmore's letter.

Sincerely,

for David E. Whitman
Arthur E. Fajans
Director
Defense Security Programs

Enclosures

cc:
Director of Policy, NSA

Appendix D: Declassification Struggle. This was the declassification situation before President Clinton's Executive order 12958 of April 1995.

PUBLIC AFFAIRS

OFFICE OF THE ASSISTANT SECRETARY OF DEFENSE
WASHINGTON, D.C. 20301-1400

FEB 27 1992
Ref: 92-0318

Mr. John E. Milmore
Post Office Box 1632
FDR Station
New York, NY 10150

Dear Mr. Milmore:

This is in response to your January 21, 1992, letter concerning an account of your experiences prior to and during the Korean War.

The National Security Agency has advised that the information in your three-page manuscript is still classified.

Sincerely,

Walter J. E. Bodling
Chief, OSD Division
Directorate for Freedom of Information and Security Review

Information Security Oversight Office
750 17th Street, NW., Suite 530
Washington, DC 20006

August 6, 1992

Dear Mr. Milmore:

This responds to your letter of March 12, 1992, requesting the Information Security Oversight Office to review the propriety of a classification decision made by the National Security Agency (NSA) regarding a manuscript you submitted for pre-publication review.

We have conducted an independent review of NSA's classification decision and have determined that the information contained in the manuscript warrants continued classification in accordance with Executive Order 12356, Section 1.3(a)(4) and (8), and (b). Although the events described in your manuscript occurred over thirty-five years ago, current circumstances suggest that the disclosure of information in your manuscript could reasonably be expected to cause serious damage to the national security.

With respect to your inference that the NSA has classified the information solely to preclude embarrassment to the U.S. Government, we found no evidence that this has occurred. Rather, the information appears to have been classified for clearly appropriate reasons.

Sincerely,

Steven Garfinkel

Steven Garfinkel
Director

Mr. John E. Milmore
P.O. Box 1632, FDR Station
New York, NY 10150

United States Senate
SELECT COMMITTEE ON INTELLIGENCE
WASHINGTON, DC 20510-6475

February 26, 1992

Mr. John Milmore
P. O. Box 1632
FDR Station
New York, NY 10150

Dear Mr. Milmore:

Thank you for contacting me to express your concerns about 18 U.S.C. sec. 798 and Executive Order 12356. I appreciate this opportunity to respond to your views.

As you are probably aware, Director of Central Intelligence Robert M. Gates has made a number of public statements on the need to increase "openness" in U.S. intelligence. This, of necessity, would involve more public access to currently classified material.

Chairman Boren recently introduced a bill, S. 2198, to substantially reorganize the U.S. intelligence community. The Committee has already had its initial public hearing on the bill, with more to come. The National Security Agency, like all other constituent agencies of the Intelligence Community, is included in our reorganization review efforts.

The end of the Cold War has prompted this re-examination of the structures and practices that were developed during its course. Your suggestions concerning declassification of material and review of existing legislation are therefore timely. I have passed your letter and enclosures to the Committee's staff to enable them to take your views into account during our current review process.

I appreciate this opportunity to respond to your concerns. Please do not hesitate to contact my office again with any matters relating to the federal government.

Sincerely,

Alfonse D'Amato
United States Senator

AD:mhh

United States Senate

SELECT COMMITTEE ON INTELLIGENCE
WASHINGTON, DC 20510-6475

November 17, 1992

Mr. John Milmore

Dear Mr. Milmore:

Senator Bradley asked me to respond to your letter of October 4 since it was addressed to him as a member of the Select Committee on Intelligence and I am his designated assistant on the Committee's staff.

I sympathize with your concern that law-abiding citizens may be deprived of their freedom of speech by arguably unduly restrictive statutes intended to protect intelligence sources or methods.

I also appreciate your interests in seeking relief from the law that bars the disclosure of information that could harm communications intelligence security, no matter how long ago the events were that the information describes.

Despite your thoughtful suggestion, the Congress did not have an opportunity to consider fully possible changes in the law this year. Still, the incoming Administration will need to draft and issue a new Executive Order to implement recently enacted statutes governing the Intelligence Community, including NSA.

In so doing, the Administration could consider changing the requirements for pre-publication review of materials which describe events over 40 years ago, such as your account of U.S. communications intelligence in Korea before and during the war.

Even if it decides not to change the the requirements, the Freedom of Information Act (FOIA) does impose a burden on

Mr. John Milmore
November 17, 1992
Page two

intelligence agencies that deny requests for declassifying documents. So, You might want to consider filing FOIA requests for documents in archives that contain the information you have been trying to have released through the pre-publication review process. While this may take some time, it is more promising because it shifts the burden of justification from you to the agencies that would deny your request.

I hope you find a way to tell your story before too long, without abandoning your legal scruples.

Sincerely,

John Despres

March 15, 1993

Freedom of Information Unit
National Security Agency
Fort George G. Meade, Maryland 20755

Dear Sir/Madam:

At the suggestion of the Senate Select Committee on Intelligence, I am submitting a request under the provisions of the Freedom of Information Act. This request includes documents, that may or may not exist, that are referred to in a three-page manuscript that was submitted to the Department of Defense for pre-publication review, that your agency advised as still classified.

I am specifically requesting an inventory of all intercepted, encrypted messages that emanated from the North Korean Peoples Army (NKPA) from its establishment in November 1949 up to the start of hostilities on June 25, 1950.

This information should have been included in testimony contained in the "Brownell Committee Report" of June 13, 1952. This report was the product of The National Security Council survey of Communications Intelligence that resulted in the creation of your agency. According to my personal recollection at least sixty items existed.

Please let me know the cost of searching for and copying a single intercept, decryption and translation. Alternatively, since the material would be 43 years old, if the documents are destroyed, archived or not in existence, I will endeavor to acquire them from other sources.

I assume your agency will comply with the provisions of the Freedom of Information Act as to statutory time limits on response and right of appeal. If you require further information please feel free to call me at 908-

Sincerely,
John E. Milmore
John E. Milmore

Copy:
United States Senate Select Committee on Intelligence
United States House of Representatives,
Permanent Select Committee on Intelligence

Enclosures-copies of letters:
Office of The Assistant Secretary of Defense, February 27,1992
Information Security Oversight Office, August 6,1992

NATIONAL SECURITY AGENCY
CENTRAL SECURITY SERVICE
FORT GEORGE G. MEADE, MARYLAND 20755-6000

Serial: J9214-93
11 June 1993

John E. Milmore

Dear Mr. Milmore:

This is in response to your Freedom of Information Act (FOIA) request of 15 March 1993 in which you asked for documents referred to in a three-page manuscript submitted to the Department of Defense.

We have determined that the fact of the existence or non-existence of the materials you request is a currently and properly classified matter in accordance with Executive Order 12356. Thus, your request is denied pursuant to the first exemption of the FOIA which provides that the FOIA does not apply to matters that are specifically authorized under criteria established by an Executive Order to be kept secret in the interest of national defense or foreign relations and are in fact properly classified pursuant to such Executive Order.

In addition, this Agency is authorized by various statutes to protect certain information concerning its activities. The third exemption of the FOIA provides for the withholding of information specifically protected from disclosure by statute. Thus, your request is also denied because the fact of the existence or non-existence of the information is exempted from disclosure pursuant to the third exemption. The specific statutes applicable in this case are Title 18 U.S. Code 798; Title 50 U.S. Code 403(d)(3); and Section 6, Public Law 86-36 (50 U.S. Code 402 note).

As your request is being denied, you are hereby advised of this Agency's appeal procedures. Any person denied access to information may, within 60 days after notification of the denial, file an appeal to the NSA/CSS Freedom of Information Act Appeal Authority. The appeal shall be in writing addressed to the NSA/CSS FOIA Appeal Authority, National Security Agency, Fort George G. Meade, MD 20755-6000. The appeal shall reference the initial denial of access and shall contain, in sufficient detail and particularity, the grounds upon which the requester believes release of the information is required. The NSA/CSS Appeal Authority will respond to the appeal within 20 working days after receipt.

Sincerely,

Linda J. Miller
for MICHAEL A. SMITH
Director of Policy

August 9, 1993

NSA/CSS Freedom of Information Appeal Authority
National Security Agency
Fort George G. Meade, MD 20755-6000

Dear Sir/Madam:

Under the provisions of the Freedom of Information Act and the procedures of your Agency, an appeal is submitted from a denial of access dated 11 June 1993 (Serial: J9214-93).

Aside from the fact that the events described occurred 43 years ago, the submitted manuscript contains no information of a revelatory cryptanalytic or sensitive procedural nature. Any personnel mentioned are either retired or deceased, and all military units indicated no longer exist.

There exist publications relating to the same subject, such as page 171 of "Korea - The Forgotten War" by Clay Blair (1987) and accounts of the trial of Joseph S. Petersen, jr. that mention the Chinese Telegraphic Code and traffic analysis of North Korean Political Security Traffic.

As to the existence or non-existence of the material requested, intercepts emanating from North Korea prior to June 25, 1950, it is my contention that all was deliberately destroyed. This was done to obviate embarrassment from an investigation that would have revealed the existence of messages indicating the precise time and locations of the North Korean invasion.

I feel that it is of compelling public interest to know that in 1950 it was the policy of the U. S. Army Security Agency not to disseminate valuable intelligence for purely petty, bureaucratic reasons. This withheld information may well have contributed to increased casualties and fatalities among U. S. forces during the Korean War. Furthermore, since NSA absorbed the personnel, facilities and procedures of that agency in 1952, did such a policy continue.

Although Public Law 86-36 virtually excludes your Agency from the burden of the Freedom of Information Act, is it at all possible to delineate in sufficient detail and particularity the grounds for denying release of the above information?

Sincerely, John E. Milmore

John E. Milmore

Enclosures: Request, Denial and page 171
"Korea - The Forgotten War".

December 27, 1993

The Honorable Bill Bradley
United States Senate
731 Hart Senate Office Building
Washington, DC 20510

Dear Senator Bradley:

Last October I wrote to you concerning a law that bars disclosure of information about or derived from communications intelligence. Your staff assistant on the Select Committee on Intelligence, Mr. John Despres was kind enough to reply and suggest I file a Freedom of Information Act request.

Although I was pessimistic at the time, and exceedingly so at present, a FOIA request was submitted to the National Security Agency. It was summarily denied, and I subsequently appealed on August 9th of this year.

NSA's FOIA Appeal Authority should have responded within twenty working days. In the absence of any reply, I have today brought this to the attention of the Director, Admiral John M. McConnell.

NSA's cavalier and dilatory approach in dealing with the public requests under the FOIA is frequently mentioned in the media, particularly in the technological area of computer data encryption techniques.

It would be appreciated if you could be of assistance in this matter as well as forwarding the enclosed information to your former committee. The telephone number of NSA's General Counsel/FOIA Appeal Authority is 301-688-6705. A Federal District Court Judge will not accept a FOIA complaint until all administrative remedies have been exhausted.

Although President Clinton is reportedly preparing a new Executive Order to govern classified information, the Communications Intelligence Security Act (Title 18, Sec. 798) should be revised to parallel or complement. This would be most necessary in the time limits set for disclosure of formerly classified information.

I suggest two further additions; punitive provisions for destroying intelligence information to preclude embarrassment to a person or Agency; falsely classifying this fact or intelligence for the same reasons. The fines and or imprisonment (present maximums $100,000 and a ten year sentence) should be commensurate with those for inadvertent disclosures or those of a "whistle blower".

Better yet, repeal the act, as it is a vestigial dinosaur of the Cold War, and permit contractual nondisclosure agreements to control sensitive information. Form 4193 has been required since 1981, with the Title 18/798 penalties imbedded in the fine print, even though the signer hasn't the remotest connection with communications intelligence activities.

If there are any questions, please feel free to call me at home (908

Sincerely,

John E. Milmore

John E. Milmore

Enclosures: Letter from John Despres,
Senate Select Committee on Intelligence
November 17, 1992
FOIA Request, March 15, 1993
NSA Denial, June 11, 1993
Appeal, August 9, 1993
Letter to the Director, NSA,
December 27, 1993

United States Senate
WASHINGTON, D.C. 20510

March 17, 1994

Mr. John E. Milmore

Dear Mr. Milmore:

Thank you for writing to express your support for additions to a proposed Execution Order regarding the Communications Intelligence Security Act. I appreciated hearing from you.

As a United States Senator, I value the thoughts and opinions I hear from concerned citizens such as yourself. This information helps me to serve both New Jersey and the nation. Your insights will be helpful to me when this issue comes before the Senate.

In the meantime, I hope you will continue to contact me on this or other matters of mutual concern. I welcome your comments.

Sincerely,

Bill Bradley
United States Senator

BB/tcz

NATIONAL SECURITY AGENCY
FORT GEORGE G. MEADE, MARYLAND 20755-6000

Serial: .9214A-93
18 March 1994

Mr. John E. Milmore

Dear Mr. Milmore:

This replies to your letter appealing the National Security Agency's (NSA) response to your request under the Freedom of Information Act (FOIA) for "an inventory of all intercepted, encrypted messages that emanated from the North Korean People's Army (NKPA) from its establishment in November 1949 up to the start of hostilities on June 25, 1950". You also requested documents that "may or may not exist" that are referred to in the three page manuscript you submitted for prepublication review.

A careful review of your original request, the Director of Policy's response to you, and your appeal were conducted. As a result of that review, a thorough search was done. As a result of that search, I have determined that no inventories of the type you requested exist and no responsive records were found.

As your appeal is denied, you are hereby advised of your rights under 5 U.S.C. § 552 to seek judicial review of this determination. You may seek an order from the United States District Court in the district in which you live, in which you have your principal place of business, in which the Agency's records are situated (U.S. District Court of Maryland), or in the District of Columbia, for review of the Agency's actions with respect to your request. Title 5 U.S.C. § 552(a)(4)(B) sets out your rights in this matter with respect to such judicial action.

Sincerely,

WILLIAM P. CROWELL
Freedom of Information/Privacy Act
Appeals Authority

--The above finding is directly contradicted below in extracts from the "official history" of the Korean War produced by the Cryptologic Museum at Fort Meade, Maryland adjacent to the National Security Agency---

Some North Korean communications were intercepted between May 1949 and April 1950 because the operators were using Soviet communications procedures. Coverage was dropped once analysts confirmed the non-Soviet origin of the material. These messages, it should be noted, were not positively identified as originating from the DPRK until after the war began and there was a basis for comparison with confirmed Korean traffic.

In April 1950, ASA undertook a limited "search and development" study of DPRK traffic. Two positions were assigned intercept of internal North Korean communications, and approximately 200 messages were on hand at the time the war began, although none had been processed.

. . . . . .

In 1952, when personnel levels and a more static war allowed some retrospective analysis, AFSA reviewed unprocessed intercept from the June 1950 period. Analysts could not find any message which would have given advance warning of the North Korean invasion. One of the earliest, if not the earliest, messages relating to the war, dated June 27 but not translated until October, referred to division level movement by North Korean forces.

The Korean War: The SIGINT Background

David A. Hatch
with
Robert Louis Benson

Introduction

Since the revelation of the vital role of cryptology in World War II, the contribution of communications intelligence (COMINT) and communications security (COMSEC) in postwar conflicts has become a frequent question for many, particularly scholars and veterans' groups.

This short summary of the cryptologic background to the Korean War is intended to provide only a general overview of the conflict from a cryptologic perspective and give initial answers to some of the more important questions about intelligence support.

This paper has been cobbled together from summaries prepared during or immediately after the period of hostilities, some original documents, and the memories of some of the participants. Some of the materials on which this history is based may not be declassified by its publication date (June 2000). I have prepared the booklet in this unusual manner in order to have a general history in time for the 50th anniversary of the beginning of the war.

NATIONAL SECURITY AGENCY
CENTRAL SECURITY SERVICE
FORT GEORGE G. MEADE, MARYLAND 20755-6000

Serial: J9142-96
19 December 1996

Mr. John E. Milmore

Dear Mr. Milmore:

This is in response to your Freedom of Information Act (FOIA) request dated 26 February 1996 for the Brownell Committee Report and related documents. In processing your request, we will conduct an Agency-wide search of our files. For the purpose of fee assessment, you have been placed in the "all other" category for this request. For your convenience, a copy of your request is enclosed.

Although the Brownell Committee Report was available without extensive search, we estimate that the cost involved to search for the remaining records you requested will be approximately $125.00. In accordance with DoD Regulation 5400.7-R, the manual search fee is computed at $25.00 an hour. If you authorize us to proceed with this search, please be advised that 5 U.S.C. 552 (4)(A)(iv)(II) allows two hours of the search and the duplication of 100 pages at no cost to you. Therefore, your total cost will be approximately $75.00. Be advised that NSA regulations and Department of Justice guidelines preclude the conducting of partial searches.

Please be advised that your agreeing to incur these fees will not necessarily result in the disclosure to you of any information. If records are found which are responsive to your request, a detailed review to determine the releasability of the information would follow. It has been our experience that any records responsive to your request, if such records exist, may still be classified or otherwise exempt from release in accordance with the exemption provisions of the FOIA. The application of these exemptions to NSA information has been consistently approved by the Federal Judiciary.

We are, therefore, suspending processing of your request pending receipt of your certified check or money order within 30 days of the date of this letter made payable to the Treasurer of the United States in the amount of $75.00 or a statement regarding your willingness to pay all assessable fees. In addition, you should be aware that this estimate is only for the fees associated with a search for documents responsive to your request. It does not include the cost of duplicating any records, in excess of 100 pages, which may be released to you.

Serial: J 9142-96

Copying costs are $.15 per page, as allowed by the DoD regulation. Addressing your correspondence to the FOIA office and adding the serial number of this letter to your check or money order will ensure proper crediting of your account.

Sincerely,

DANIEL E. BARCHANOWICZ
Chief
FOIA/PA Services

Encl:
a/s

NATIONAL SECURITY AGENCY
CENTRAL SECURITY SERVICE
FORT GEORGE G. MEADE, MARYLAND 20755-6000

Serial: J9142A-96
7 January 1997

Mr. John E. Milmore

Dear Mr. Milmore:

We are in receipt of your letter dated 1 January 1997 in which you forwarded advance payment of $75.00 with regard to your FOIA request dated 26 February 1996 for the Brownell Committee Report and related documents. In you letter you advise us that the payment "is to expedite the processing" of your request. It appears that our letter of 19 December 1996 in which we advise you of the estimated search costs related to this request was not clear and you believe that by agreeing to pay the estimated search fee your FOIA request will be expedited. Please be advised that a FOIA request may be expedited only when it is demonstrated that (1) an individual's life or personal safety would be jeopardized by failure to process a request immediately; (2) the substantial due process rights of the requester would be impaired by the failure to process the request immediately and the information sought is not otherwise available; and (3) other narrowly construed exceptional circumstances exist. Your request does not meet the criteria set forth above; therefore, the processing of your request will not be expedited.

NSA processes requests on a two-track queue: first-in, first-out and easy-hard. This method of responding to requesters is advocated by both the Department of Defense, of which NSA is a component, and the Department of Justice. The first-in, first-out system is employed in fairness to all requesters. When we acknowledged receipt of your initial request of 26 February 1996, we also notified you that 403 cases preceded it in the queue. As our postcard explains, the complexity, volume, and sensitivity of the records, as well as the potential need to consult with other agencies, will affect the amount of time it takes to respond to requesters. Regarding the easy-hard processing, we believe it is needless for a requester to wait a long period of time to learn that the Agency has no records responsive to his request or to obtain records that do not require a lengthy review. In your case, the records require considerable review and your request does not constitute an "easy" one. Therefore, your request remains in queue and will be processed in order. Because of the variables anticipated in the processing of your request, as well as those "hard" requests preceding yours in the queue, we are unable to provide you with a completion date.

Serial: J9142A-96

This information is being conveyed to you to enable you to better understand the status of your request and to advise you that your money order is being held pending notification from you advising us if you wish to pursue this request. Please advise us within 30 days of the date of this letter if you are still interested in receiving the requested material although processing will not be expedited. If you are still interested in pursuing your request it will be processed in order as indicated above. If no response is received within 30 days of the date of this letter, we will assume you no longer require this information, processing will be discontinued and your $75.00 advance payment will be refunded to you.

Sincerely,

DANIEL E. BARCHANOWICZ
Chief
FOIA/PA Branch

NATIONAL SECURITY AGENCY
CENTRAL SECURITY SERVICE
FORT GEORGE G. MEADE, MARYLAND 20755-6000

Serial: J9142B-96

30 AUG 1999

Mr. John E. Milmore

Dear Mr. Milmore:

This is in response to your telecon with my representative, Georgia, on 24 August 1999, as to the status of your Freedom of Information Act request, dated 26 February 1996, for the Brownell Committee Report. We sent you a letter (enclosed) dated 7 January 1997 acknowledging receipt of your $75.00 payment and informing you that we were unable to provide you with a completion date at that time. On 16 April 1999, you spoke with another one of my representatives who informed you that we anticipate processing your case in the year 2002.

We appreciate your continued patience.

Sincerely,

Barbara Paisley

BARBARA PAISLEY
Chief,
FOIA/PA Services

Encl:
a/s

NATIONAL SECURITY AGENCY
CENTRAL SECURITY SERVICE
FORT GEORGE G. MEADE, MARYLAND 20755-6000

FOIA Case: 8185
30 November 2001

Mr. John E. Milmore

Dear Mr. Milmore:

This responds to your Freedom of Information Act (FOIA) request of 26 February 1996 for "1) Brownell Committee Report of June 13, 1952, 2) Supporting documents and transcripts of interviews by Messrs. Benjamin R. Shute, Lloyd N. Cutler, Harmon Duncombe and Grant C. Manson, and 3) any reports, recommendations, and cables from AFSA team which visited Tokyo in July 1950 at the request of General McArthur's HQ...." Your request has been assigned case number 8185 and has been processed under the FOIA. Regarding item 1 of your request (Brownell Committee Report of June 13, 1952), we have enclosed a copy of this report. Certain information, however, has been deleted.

Some of the information deleted from the enclosed document was found to be currently and properly classified in accordance with Executive Order 12958. This information meets the criteria for classification as set forth in Subparagraphs (c), (d), and (g) of Section 1.5 and remains classified TOP SECRET as provided in Section 1.3 of Executive Order 12958. The information is classified because its disclosure could reasonably be expected to exceptionally grave damage to the national security. The information is exempt from automatic declassification in accordance with Section 3.4(b) of Executive Order 12958. Because the information is currently and properly classified, it is exempt from disclosure pursuant to the first exemption of the FOIA (5 U.S.C. Section 552(b)(1)).

In addition, this Agency is authorized by various statutes to protect certain information concerning its activities. We have determined that such information exists in these documents. Accordingly, those portions are also exempt from disclosure pursuant to the third exemption of the FOIA that provides for the withholding of information specifically protected from disclosure by statute. The specific statutes applicable in this case are Title 18 U.S. Code 798; Title 50 U.S. Code 403-3(c)(6); and Section 6, Public Law 86-36 (50 U.S. Code 402 note).

Regarding item 2 (Supporting documents and transcripts of interviews by Messrs. Benjamin R. Shute, Lloyd N. Cutler, Harmon Duncombe and Grant C. Manson) and item 3 (any reports, recommendations, and cables from AFSA team which visited Tokyo in July 1950 at the request of General McArthur's HQ) of your request, please be advised that we were unable to locate any records responsive to these portions of your request.

Since the deletions in the enclosed document and/or our inability to locate records responsive to items 2 and 3 of your request may be construed as a partial denial of your request, you are hereby advised of this Agency's appeal procedures. Any person denied access to information may file an appeal to the NSA/CSS Freedom of Information Act Appeal Authority. The appeal must be postmarked no later than 60 calendar days from the date of the initial denial letter. The appeal shall be in writing addressed to the NSA/CSS FOIA Appeal Authority (DC321), National Security Agency, 9800 Savage Road STE 6248, Fort George G. Meade, MD 20755-6248. The appeal shall reference the initial denial of access and shall contain, in sufficient detail and particularity, the grounds upon which the requester believes release of the information is required. The NSA/CSS Appeal Authority will endeavor to respond to the appeal within 20 working days after receipt, absent any unusual circumstances.

Please be advised that enclosed document contains information which originated with other government agencies. Because we are unable to make determinations as to the releasability of the other agencies' information, the subject document has been referred to the appropriate agencies for review. We will respond to you further when consultation with the other agencies has been completed.

Sincerely,

Sally V. Seward

SALLY V. SEWARD
Deputy Director of Policy

Encl:
a/s

It should be helpful, at this stage, to illustrate how the exemption of particular Service intercept facilities from AFSA's "operational direction" has affected the employment of our total intercept capabilities. In the several months preceding the invasion of Korea in June, 1950, the U. S. had some [ ] intercept positions so situated as to be capable of intercepting North Korean traffic. Of these [ ] positions, AFSA had "operational direction" of [ ] the remainder being directed by the Army and Air Force. AFSA had many other demands for the limited facilities available to it, and assigned only [ ] of the [ ] positions to search for and intercept North Korean traffic. In large part because only [ ] positions were assigned to the task, AFSA was [ ] no Korean traffic whatever at the time of the invasion in June, 1950. With the benefit of hindsight, it is now clear that it would have been wiser to assign more of the [ ] available positions to Korean traffic. If AFSA had had the [ ] positions under its operational direction, it might still have decided for what seemed to be good reasons in the Spring of 1950 that [ ] were sufficient to cover North Korea. But AFSA never had the opportunity to decide how many positions it would put on Korea out of [ ] AFSA had only [ ] positions under its control.

After the invasion in June 1950, both AFSA and the Services rapidly assigned a considerable number of intercept positions to North Korean traffic. Some [ ] North Korean encrypted and plain text messages were intercepted

FOIA(b)1
FOIA(b)3 - 50 USC 403
FOIA(b)3 - 18 USC 798
FOIA(b)3 - P.L. 86-36 sec 6

in July, and by September the monthly total had risen to [ ] But despite an impressive increase in total effort, the division of "operational direction" among the Services and AFSA led to a number of wasteful and inefficient practices. The Army (ASAPAC) and Air Force (AFSS) units in the theater duplicated much of their intercept effort on Soviet and [ ] traffic in the combat areas, with neither unit accomplishing complete coverage or analysis on either problem. Despite the urgent recommendations of an AFSA team (which visited the theater at the invitation of General MacArthur's headquarters) that ASAPAC and AFSS divide and coordinate their efforts by agreement, the duplication continued for an additional year until ASAPAC voluntarily discontinued its own efforts on both problems in March of 1952. Similarly, AFSA recommended in the Spring of 1951 that the direction finding (D/F) facilities and activities of the three Services in the Far East be placed under common control to obtain results on [ ] traffic that were urgently needed and could not be achieved with the limited facilities possessed by any one Service. The Committee is advised that this single and obvious step was not adopted until this Spring, more than a year after the original recommendation was made. And today, despite a substantial increase in the number of intercept positions in the Western Pacific, the proportion under AFSA operational direction has actually declined, from [ ] out of [ ] in June 1950 to [ ] out of [ ] on May 1, 1952.

FOIA(b)1
FOIA(b)3 - 50 USC 403
FOIA(b)3 - 18 USC 798
FOIA(b)3 - P.L. 86-36 sec 6

NATIONAL SECURITY AGENCY
CENTRAL SECURITY SERVICE
FORT GEORGE G. MEADE, MARYLAND 20755-6000

FOIA Case: 8185
24 April 2002

Mr. John E. Milmore

Dear Mr. Milmore:

This responds to your 21 March 2002 letter requesting a refund for the information you received as the result of a Freedom of Information Act (FOIA) request for "1) Brownell Committee Report of June 13, 1952, 2) Supporting documents and transcripts of interviews by Messrs. Benjamin R. Shute, Lloyd N. Cutler, Harmon Duncombe and Grant C. Manson, and 3) any reports, recommendations, and cables from AFSA team which visited Tokyo in July 1950 at the request of General McArthur's HQ...." Your request was assigned case number 8185 and was processed under the FOIA.

In your recent letter you note your disapproval with the copy of the Brownell Committee Report that you received, since it was not "unredacted." We understand your frustration; however, as we indicated in our response to you, some of the information in the document remains currently and properly classified and cannot be released. In addition, we are still waiting for responses from other agencies regarding the review of their information. Once those responses are received, it is likely that some additional information will be released to you. There is no provision in the FOIA for refunding search fees when the results of the search are not what the requester anticipated.

The $75.00 fee that you paid represented the estimated costs associated with conducting a search for material responsive to all three portions of your request. In our 19 December 1996 correspondence to you, we informed you that the cost involved to search for the records you requested would be approximately $125.00. Allowing you 2 hours of search for free as an "all other" requester, your total search cost was estimated to be $75.00. Following receipt of your recent letter, we noticed that the actual search costs had not been reported to you. The actual search for materials responsive to your request took 2 hours. Because the FOIA allows you 2 free hours of search,

FOIA Case: 8185

there are no search fees associated with the processing of your case. A refund of your search fees should have been provided to you with our 30 November 2002 response. Your advance payment of $75.00 will be refunded to you under separate cover.

Sincerely,

PAMELA N. PHILLIPS
Chief
FOIA/PA Services

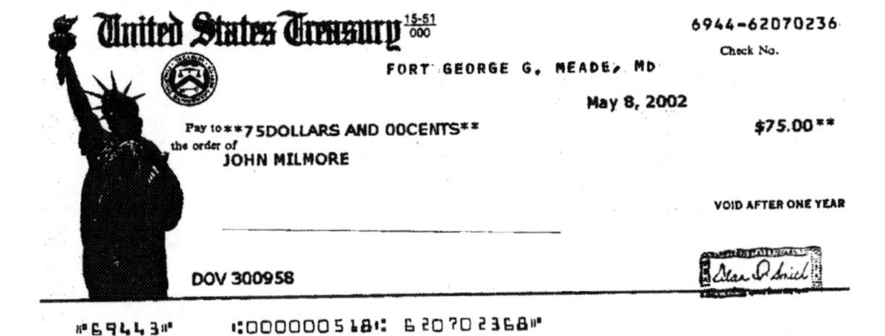

United States Treasury 15-51/000

6944-62070236
Check No.

FORT GEORGE G. MEADE, MD

May 8, 2002

Pay to the order of **75DOLLARS AND 00CENTS** $75.00**

JOHN MILMORE

VOID AFTER ONE YEAR

DOV 300958

⑈6944 3⑈ ⑆000000518⑆ 62070236 8⑈

Appendix D:

The entire history of American communications intelligence - "Codebreaking" is rather spotty in spite of exaggerated claims of miraculous accomplishments.

In WW I William Frederick Friedman served with a small U. S. Army unit in France that was subsequently disbanded. He stayed on in the Army Signal Corps and did much original research into cryptography and produced many valuable military textbooks on the subject.

In the interim period between wars, Herbert Osborne Yardley headed up a civilian entity dubbed "The American Black Chamber" that was located on East 37th Street in Manhattan. This also became the title of his sensational book, written to expose the closing down of the "Chamber" in 1929 by Secretary of State Henry

Stimson because "Gentlemen do not read each other's mail". The book informed the Japanese Government the Americans were reading their diplomatic codes.

In Shanghai, as early as 1923 the U. S. Navy set up a radio intercept post atop the American consulate building. Affectionately nicknamed the "up on the roof gang" its first task was to monitor the movements of the Japanese Navy.

The Army Signal Corps disguised the 2nd Signal Service Company as a radio intercept intelligence unit. The first intercept station was based at Fort Hancock on Sandy Hook, New Jersey. These activities segued into the breaking of the Japanese Diplomatic encryption system dubbed either "Purple" or "Magic", as well as partial decryption of the Japanese Naval code and the subsequent intelligence fiasco at Pearl Harbor.

World War II was a hit or miss affair, with sometimes-excellent intelligence from deciphered Axis communications, but at other times there was complete blackouts. Both the Navy and Army had many intercept stations scattered across the globe led by the U.S. Army's SIS (Signal Intelligence Service).

After the Big War the thrust of activity was directed towards the Soviet Union and the Eastern Block countries. Headquarters Army Security Agency Pacific was activated on November 25, 1945 at Manila, Philippine Islands. Colonel Abraham Sinkov was designated Acting Chief ASAPAC. He was an expert cryptanalyst who had received the order of The British Empire among other decorations. He returned to Arlington Hall as a civilian and was succeeded by Colonel Collins as ASAPAC moved to Tokyo on May 6, 1946. At first ASAPAC was lodged in the "Forestry Building" in downtown Tokyo's financial district but subsequently moved to the First Tokyo Arsenal in the northern ward of the metropolis with an authorized strength of 50 officers and 175 enlisted men. It remained under the direct control of the War Department the predecessor of the Department of the Army. It never was under the control of General MacArthur's GHQ as far as operations, training or the assignment, transfer and promotion of personnel.

The Berlin Airlift of 1948 caused a build-up of radio intercept units led by the British with the 26th Signals Company at Gatow airfield in Berlin followed by the Americans with units at Hertzogenaurach in Germany, Asmara in Eriteria, and numerous stations in the Far East - Philippines and occupied Japan. The Korean War caused a massive increase of Army and Navy communications intelligence capabilities, as well as in the Air Force with the introduction of airborne electronic signal interceptors.

The Viet Nam war was bollixed up from the beginning with the "Tonkin Gulf Resolution" that stemmed from the misreading of North Vietnamese naval messages. This was admitted by the National Security Agency, one year after the erroneous Viet Namese "Tonkin Gulf - Second Attack" intercepted messages was first presented to President Johnson. There was no second attack; the damage had already been done as America was in a full-scale war, the war that almost tore the country apart.

The intelligence failure that resulted in the events of September 11, 2001 was monumental. In James Bamford's recent book, published in May of that year, he revealed that NSA was bragging about intercepting Osama Bin Laden's INTMARSAT telephone conversations. Appraised of this fact, Bin Laden stopped using that mode of communication. If this information was properly and legally kept under wrap, could the attacks on the World Trade Center and the Pentagon been anticipated and prevented?

GLOSSARY AND ACRONYMS

Additive A numeric encryption method of adding numbers to a code or cipher.

AFSA Armed Forces Security Agency, a short term 1949 to 1952 predecessor to NSA.

AFSS . Air Force Security Service

ASA. . Army Security Agency (1946-1978) .The branch of the U. S. Army responsible for COMINT and cryptographic security.

CCF.. Chinese Communist Forces. U. S. Military designation, also Chinese volunteers.

CIA. . Central Intelligence Agency. Formed in 1948 to coordinate all intelligence gathering, Successor to the OSS (Office of Strategic Services).

Cryptanalysis. .The process of determining the content of encrypted messages.

COMINT . Communications Intelligence. In general any information gathered from transmissions, specifically cryptanalysis.

CIC. .. Counter Intelligence Corps. U. S. Army HUMINT organization.

CSA.. Communications Supplementary Activities.U. S. Navy COMINT organization, 1950's.

CRC.. Communications Reconnaissance Company. See SSC.

CTC . Chinese Telegraphic Code. Commercially available 10,000-group numeric code to represent Chinese ideographs, around since early 1900's, The "Ming" code.

D/F Radio Direction Finding.

ELINT . Electronic Intelligence. Particular COMINT such as intercepting RADAR or telemetry.

ENIGMA a German electromechanical rotor encryption machine used during World War II,

EUSAK.. . Eighth United States Army Korea

FEAF . . . Far East Air Force

FEC. . . . . Far East Command

G-2 . . . .. General Staff Officer for Intelligence

G-3 .. General Staff Officer for Operations

GHQ . General Headquarters

HUMINT . . Human Intelligence (spies, other sources)

INSCOM . Intelligence and Security Command, Successor to ASA in 1970's.

KMAG . . . Korean Military Advisory Group. Principal U. S. Army liaison to ROK army.

MAGIC. . American code word for Japanese COMINT. Usually intelligence from Japanese diplomatic messages, but later any COMINT.

MOS Military Occupation Specialty. Prior to 1951 a three-digit code for an enlisted man's profession, Four-digit later.

NavSecGrup . . Naval Security Group, see CSA

NKPA North Korean Peoples Army, Sometimes KPA or "In-Min-Gun".

NSA National Security Agency. Founded in 1952 to provide COMINT and cryptographic service to the Departments of Defense and State.

RCT Regimental Combat Team. Basic combat organization of the U. S. Army, Infantry,. .artillery and sometimes armor.

ROK . Republic of Korea

SIGINT Signal Intelligence See traffic analysis, but sometimes refers to COMINT.

SIS . Signal Intelligence Service The predecessor of ASA (1940-1945)

SSC. . Signal Service Company, An Army Mobile Radio Intelligence gathering unit. Later became CRC.

SSD. . Signal Service Detachment, A smaller SSC, For radio direction finding or communications monitoring for security.

Traffic Analysis, Intelligence derived from all components of radio intercept activity other than cryptanalysis.

ULTRA British Code Word for European COMINT Usually applied to ENIGMA decrypts, but applied generically to all COMINT.

VENONA . Code word for translations of Soviet Espionage messages. (also called BRIDE).

Additional Photographs

July 28, 1951. Tokyo, HQ ASAPAC. Award of the Bronze Star Col. Edwin Greiner, Cpl. John Milmore, Capt. Ben McKibben.

July 28, 1951. Tokyo, HQ ASAPAC. Reviewing the Troops.
The 293rd Army Band. Lt. Col. Clarence Sills, Cpl. Milmore
Color Guard: Sargents Miller, Weik, Rumery and Lormand.

July 28, 1951. Tokyo, ASAPAC. Lt. Col Sills, Cpl. Milmore